THE REMINISCENCES OF Vice Admiral Robert Taylor Scott Keith U.S. Navy (Retired)

INTERVIEWED BY
Paul Stillwell

U.S. Naval Institute • Annapolis, Maryland

Copyright © 1996

Preface

During his nearly 40 years in Navy uniform, Vice Admiral Taylor Keith bore witness to dramatic changes in the Navy's capability to carry out its missions. When he first went to sea in the mid-1920s, it was in a coal-fired battleship armed with guns that could barely shoot over the horizon. When he retired four decades later, he was in command of a fleet that included guided missile frigates armed with the latest in electronic equipment and aircraft carriers whose planes could reach out hundreds of miles.

Taylor Keith, a Virginian, came from a line of lawyers. Early in life, though, he determined he wanted to follow a different career path. He opted for the Naval Academy, and during the course of his commissioned service he had three further tours of duty in Annapolis. He took it as his mission to help shape the lives of hundreds of future officers, just as his own had been shaped by his experiences as a midshipman.

As a naval warrior, Keith's efforts were concentrated primarily in battleships and destroyers. In the memoir that follows, he traces his career growth as an officer. When he was an ensign in the battleship Utah in 1928, his ship carried President-elect Herbert Hoover during a goodwill journey to South America. As a vice admiral in 1963, Admiral Keith's First Fleet put on an impressive guided-missile firepower demonstration for the benefit of another President, John F. Kennedy.

In between, he underwent duty in a series of increasingly responsible billets. Included was command of the Fletcher-class destroyer Nicholas as she demonstrated capability in both antisubmarine warfare and naval gunnery during the campaign to wrest the Pacific from the Japanese. Particularly noteworthy was the destroyer's duel with a submarine armed with manned suicide torpedoes. A decade later, Keith had the honor of commanding the battleship Missouri, then the most notable surface combatant in the fleet.

Throughout his years of service, working with thousands of officers and enlisted men, Keith consistently demonstrated the principles of leadership, especially loyalty downward. In this memoir he is becomingly modest, even poking fun at himself at times. He gives the credit to those who worked for him in a variety of jobs. The only regret about the oral history is that the limited time available for the interviews did not permit him to go into greater detail in discussing his career.

When he was telling of his various duties, Admiral Keith frequently jumped from one subject to another, rather than covering his career in systematic, chronological fashion. Therefore, for the benefit of the readers, the contents have been rearranged to put the material into sequence. This finished version has the blessing of Mrs. Keith. Researchers interested in seeing the original, unedited transcripts may do so at the Naval Institute. In the completion of this volume, Ms. Ann Hassinger of the Naval Institute's history division has made a significant contribution through her diligence in the overall process of printing, proofreading, and overseeing the binding.

Paul Stillwell
Director, History Division
U.S. Naval Institute
April 1996

VICE ADMIRAL ROBERT TAYLOR SCOTT KEITH
UNITED STATES NAVY (RETIRED)

Robert Taylor Scott Keith was born in Washington, D.C., on 19 May 1905, son of John A. C. and Mary W. (Scott) Keith. He attended Stuyvesant School in Warrenton, Virginia, and the Severn School, Severna Park, Maryland. In 1924 he was appointed to the U.S. Naval Academy, Annapolis, Maryland, from the state of Virginia. Graduated with the degree of bachelor of science and commissioned ensign on 7 June 1928, he subsequently advanced to the rank of rear admiral, to date from 1 August 1956, and served in the temporary rank of vice admiral, from 1 May 1962 until 25 January 1964. On 1 July 1964 he was transferred to the retired list of the U.S. Navy and advanced to vice admiral, the highest rank he held while on active duty.

Following graduation from the Naval Academy in 1928, Ensign Keith remained there for the summer course in aviation, reporting in September aboard the USS Utah (BB-31). In October 1930 he was transferred to the USS Arizona (BB-39), and in March 1932 he was detached for duty in the USS Overton (DD-239). While attached to the latter, he participated in the Second Nicaraguan Campaign. Following a year's duty at sea as communications officer of the USS Nitro (AE-2), he was ordered in May 1935 to the Naval Postgraduate School, Annapolis, Maryland, to attend the course in general line.

From June 1936 to May 1937, he was assigned to the Naval Observatory in Washington, D.C., where he had instruction in time service. He next joined the staff of Commander Base Force, USS Argonne (AS-10) flagship, as aide and flag lieutenant. He continued to serve in that capacity until June 1939, when he reported as gunnery officer of the USS Aylwin (DD-355). In early 1941 he spent a few months as executive officer of the USS Cushing (DD-376). Returning to the Naval Academy in July 1941, he served in the executive department until August 1943. After completing instruction at the West Coast Sound School, San Diego, California, he assumed command of the USS Nicholas (DD-449). For outstanding service while in command of that destroyer, he received thee awards of the Legion of Merit, each with combat "V." The citations follow:

Legion of Merit: "For exceptionally meritorious conduct . . . during action against enemy Japanese forces in the Pacific War Area on November 12, 1944, when his ship established radar contact with a surfaced hostile submarine, [he] maneuvered to the area and, although the enemy vessel had submerged and was employing violent evasive tactics, succeeded in launching an attack to destroy the underseas craft . . .

Gold Star in lieu of the second Legion of Merit: "For outstanding service . . . as Commanding Officer of the USS NICHOLAS during operations against enemy Japanese forces in the Pacific War Area over a period of fourteen months. Maintaining his ship at highest standard of fighting efficiency, [he] contributed greatly to the success of his vessel during sustained operations against the Japanese from the Marshalls to Luzon . . . "

Gold star in lieu of the third Legion of Merit: "For exceptionally meritorious conduct . . . in action against enemy Japanese forces in the Pacific War Area on February 17, 1944. When his ship obtained radar contact on an enemy submarine while serving as a unit of a screening of destroyers, [he] initiated an immediate attack and, skillfully maneuvering the NICHOLAS in darkness to insure the delivery of maximum gunfire, played an important part in the probable damaging of the hostile vessel before it submerged. Then conducting a series of depth-charge attacks until sonar contact was lost, he received assurance of the probable destruction of the submarine from floating deck gratings, bubbling diesel oil and a large slick which was visible for several days . . . "

Detached from command of the Nicholas on 6 February 1945, Commander Keith was assigned briefly to the East Coast Sound School, prior to assuming command of the USS Herbert J. Thomas (DD-833). He was Commander Destroyer Division 17, USS Turner (DD-834) flagship, and later Commander Destroyer Division 32, USS Benner (DD-807) flagship, from July 1945 to May 1946, interspersed with duty during February and March 1946 in command of Destroyer Squadron Three, USS Frank Knox (DD-742) flagship. Returning to the United States, he served in the Bureau of Naval Personnel, Navy Department, Washington D.C., until June 1949, then became Commander Fleet Training Group and Underway Training Element, Pearl Harbor, Hawaii.

He served as secretary of the academic board and aide to the Superintendent of the Naval Academy between April 1950 and June 1953, when he became chief of staff and aide to Commander Destroyer Force Atlantic Fleet. In April 1954 he assumed command of the USS Missouri (BB-63), and in October of the same year returned to the Naval Academy to serve as commandant of midshipmen. After duty at sea as Commander Destroyer Flotilla Two from September 1956 until August 1957, he served until March 1959 as Commander Naval Base, Subic Bay, Luzon, Philippine Islands.

In March 1959 he assumed the duties of Assistant Chief of Naval Operations (Naval Reserve), Navy Department. After a year in that assignment, he again went to sea, this time as Commander Cruiser-Destroyer Force Pacific Fleet. In November 1961 he reported as senior member of the United Nations Command Military Armistice Commission, Seoul, Korea. On 5 May 1962, in the rank of vice admiral, he assumed command of the First Fleet. He was hospitalized from 4 December 1963 and on 1 July 1964 was transferred to the retired list of the U.S. Navy.

"For exceptionally meritorious conduct . . . during the period April 1960 through January 1964 as Commander Cruiser-Destroyer Force, U.S. Pacific Fleet; Senior Member of the United Nations Command Military Armistice Commission Korea; and Commander First Fleet . . . " he was awarded a gold star in lieu of the fourth Legion of Merit. The citation further states: "As Commander Cruiser-Destroyer Force, U.S. Pacific Fleet, [he] conceived and initiated a major reorganization of this force, the new Cruiser-Destroyer Flotilla concept, which significantly and materially improved combat readiness in tactical deployment and achieved the best balance of capabilities available. While serving as Senior Member of the United Nations Command Military Armistice Commission in Korea, he was charged with negotiating with representatives of Communist China and North Korea in any matter that was brought before the Commission. During the period, he exercised the utmost ability, tact, and grasp of international affairs in what can best be described as one of the world's most difficult political arenas. In his role as Commander FIRST Fleet, [he] displayed brilliant leadership and professional competence in maintaining the Fleet at a high level of combat readiness, developing his ships into extremely effective fighting units, individual and collectively, ready for any contingency . . . "

In addition to the Legion of Merit with three gold stars and combat "V," Vice Admiral Keith received the Second Nicaraguan Campaign Medal; the American Defense Service Medal, fleet clasp; Asiatic-Pacific Campaign Medal; American Campaign Medal; World War II Victory Medal; Navy Occupation Service Medal, Asia clasp; National Defense Service Medal; and the Philippine Liberation Ribbon.

Vice Admiral Keith was married to the former Eleanor L. Hudgins of Norfolk, Virginia. Their twin sons are Robert T. S., Keith, Jr., and Martin Langhorne Keith, born 4 November 1936. Admiral Keith died 12 February 1989 at Falls Church, Virginia.

DATES OF RANK:

Ensign, 7 June 1928
Lieutenant (junior grade), 7 June 1931
Lieutenant, 19 May 1937
Lieutenant Commander, 1 January 1942
Commander, 15 September 1942
Captain, 25 March 1945
Rear Admiral, 1 August 1956
Vice Admiral, 1 May 1962

Authorization

The U.S. Naval Institute is hereby authorized to make available to individuals, libraries, and other repositories of its choosing the transcripts of two oral history interviews concerning the life and career of the late Vice Admiral Robert Taylor Scott Keith, U.S. Navy (Retired). The interviews were recorded on 13 January 1987 and 14 January 1987 in collaboration with Paul Stillwell for the U.S. Naval Institute.

The undersigned does hereby release and assign to the U.S. Naval Institute all right, title, restrictions, and interest in the interviews. The copyright in both the oral and transcribed versions shall be the sole property of the U.S. Naval Institute. The tape recordings of the interviews are and will remain the property of the U.S. Naval Institute.

Signed and sealed this 10th day of February 1996.

_____
Mrs. Eleanor Keith, for the estate of
Vice Admiral R. T. S. Keith, USN (Ret.)

Interviews Number 1 and 2 with Vice Admiral Robert Taylor Scott Keith, U.S. Navy (Retired)

Place: Admiral Keith's home in Coronado, California

Dates: Tuesday, 13 January 1987, and Wednesday, 14 January 1987

Interviewer: Paul Stillwell

(For the sake of continuity and the convenience of readers, the following material is presented in chronological sequence rather than the order in which Admiral Keith discussed various topics in the interviews themselves.)

Q: Admiral, in the conventional fashion of these oral biographies we usually start at the beginning of the life and career. Could you please describe the events that led to your going to the Naval Academy originally?

Admiral Keith: Very briefly. I come from what I consider to be a line of lawyers. I was the son of a lawyer. One Easter vacation, when I was a schoolboy, I went into the local court, and I heard two lawyers try an automobile theft case. Into the second day of it, they had been so inept and so poor in handling the evidence they were trying to present that I went home and talked to my mother, who was raising me as a widow. I said to her, "Do I have to be a lawyer?"

She said, "No. Why do you ask?"

I said, "If I became a lawyer and had no more ability than the people I've been listening to for the last two days, I would feel I was a disgrace to my line, and I don't want to be one. I'd like to do something else."

At that time, in the 1920s, we lived in a small town, Warrenton, Virginia. In a period of a few years, several boys went from there to West Point, and several of them went to the Naval Academy. I thought that would be a good thing for me to do also. My father died when I was young and left four children; there wasn't a great deal of money. It didn't cost a great deal of money to go to school in those days, but it still cost money. So I followed along with my group and applied for the Naval Academy. I went to Severn School and learned enough mathematics to try and get through, because I wasn't then and am not now a mathematician.*

* * *

Q: You were probably in one of the last classes of midshipmen that had a coal-burning summer cruise.

Admiral Keith: Yes. I was definitely on that cruise, and I saw a great many people scuffle and push and fight to shovel the last shovel full of coal on a battleship, but I had no desire for that whatsoever.† I spent my first cruise down in the bowels of the Texas, and I hauled those coals out of there. It must have been 500 degrees, the temperature burning my tender little skin. I got inside of bunkers and struck down coal so that it would go out of the chutes. In Gibraltar I coaled ship when they dropped tons of Welsh dust on deck and called it coal. When we got through and cleaned the ship up, they decided that more of the coal had blown away than they could afford to lose and still get us home on the cruise, so we had to start in and do it all over again. Not to shovel that last shovelful of coal didn't bother me one bit in the world.

* * *

I finished the Naval Academy in 1928, and my first duty after graduation was aviation summer at the Naval Academy. There we were given some flying, not as pilots, but to learn something about being in the air. Dan Gallery was my instructor.‡ In the flying

---

* The Severn School, in Severna Park, Maryland, has been used as a preparatory school by many prospective midshipmen over the years.
† The Texas (BB-35) received a substantial modernization in 1925-26 at the Norfolk Navy Yard. Included were oil-fired boilers, tripod foremast, additional armor, and anti-torpedo blisters.
‡ Lieutenant Daniel V. Gallery, Jr., USN. While in command of the USS Guadalcanal (CVE-60) in June 1944, his forces captured the German submarine U-505. Gallery eventually became a rear admiral and wrote a number of popular books about the Navy.

boat that we were using, there was a little niche where you could look down through a window, and that's where the navigator stood. I was supposed to navigate by sight around Chesapeake Bay, pick up landmarks, and tell the pilot to fly this course and that course to get to the next landmark. All the fumes of the engine came down in there, and I was ill from the fumes. All at once, we were down on the water, and Mr. Gallery asked, "Mr. Keith, where are we?"

I said, "Indeed, Mr. Gallery, if you don't know, we're lost." [Laughter]

* * *

Then I reported to the Utah, which was in dry dock for interim bottom-scraping.[*]

Q: Was this at Boston?

Admiral Keith: No, this was in the New York Navy Yard. Two hours after I reported on board, the telephone in the JO mess rang, and it was the captain.[†] He was looking for a tennis game. Well, the only other JO on board was my Naval Academy roommate, and we both played tennis. So we went up, and I found out the other partner was to be the executive officer.

Q: Was this skipper Captain Train?

Admiral Keith: This was Captain Charles Russell Train.[‡] We had a good game, and they enjoyed our opposition. I guess we let them win easily. We played with them several times, so that I came to know my captain rather early.

The word always went back to the Naval Academy from your predecessors who had gone into the fleet. They would say, "This is a wonderful ship. This is a hell house." The Arizona on the West Coast was the worst one, and everybody stayed clear of that. The

---

[*] The USS Utah (BB-31) was commissioned in August 1911. She had a standard displacement of 21,825 tons, was 522 feet long, and 88 feet in the beam. Her top speed was 21 knots. Her main battery comprised ten 12-inch guns.
[†] JO mess--junior officers' mess.
[‡] Captain Charles R. Train, USN, commanded the battleship Utah (BB-31) from 29 August 1928 to 2 June 1930.

Utah was the worst one on the East Coast. You drew numbers, and you got your ship by the number. Those that had very high numbers got the last choices. My roommate and I both drew high numbers, and the Utah was the only thing left on the East Coast, where we wanted to be.

Q: Who was your roommate?

Admiral Keith: Gene Carusi, from Washington.*

Q: What was it about the Utah that was considered undesirable?

Admiral Keith: I never knew, except that they had a skipper who apparently was unreasonable, as far as JOs were concerned.† It's too long ago to cite any examples of what they told you his idiosyncrasies were that made duty on that ship not pleasant. There were no idiosyncrasies about Captain Train, whose advent had occurred, obviously, before I reported on board. He made it one of the happiest ships, I think, anybody ever served in.

In those days, you went to sea on Monday morning, did your training exercises off the Virginia Capes, and came in on Thursday evenings. Then most people abandoned ship and went to Baltimore or Washington for weekends on the overnight boats. You came back Sunday night, caught a boat at Old Point Comfort, went out to your ship, and went to sea.‡ Quarters in those days were at 9:15 in the morning. Breakfast was served on board ship at 8:00 o'clock. It was a very pleasant life. There was no reason to get upset with the Navy. [Laughter]

One night I was on the boat, coming back from Washington, and the captain was there with his wife, who didn't go to Norfolk. As I was standing in line to get a ticket, he walked over to me and said, "Would you get my ticket?"

---

* Ensign Eugene C. Carusi, USN.
† Captain William L. Littlefield, USN, commanded the Utah from 23 January 1927 to 29 August 1928.
‡ Old Point Comfort is a narrow spit of land at the end of a peninsula where Hampton Roads meets the Chesapeake Bay, near Norfolk, Virginia.

I said, "Yes, sir."

I took it over to him after I had gotten it, and he said, "Have dinner with me when we go down the river." So at dinner, he said, "This has been a magnificent weekend for the Utah in Washington. We have been selected to go down to Montevideo and wait for President-elect Hoover, who is going to make a goodwill tour to South America.* He will cross the Andes and come over to join us. We'll bring him back up the coast via Rio."

Q: He was going down the West Coast in the Maryland.

Admiral Keith: That's right. He was going down in the Maryland. Apparently, the Maryland wasn't too happy a cruise for the newspapermen. They were ready to let go, but they decided to wait and see what things were like on the Utah, to see if it was true that different ships, different long splices.† Apparently, they were mollified, and they didn't let blasts go at the Navy for its martinet-type command.

There, early on, I had an opportunity to have my thoughts directed to something other than everyday life. Here was a President, immediately after his election. He left in November and was gone until January, going down to South America, where he evidently felt we had great interests, and that goodwill was something that we needed and he hoped could follow upon his trip down there. Well, that makes a young person start to think really a little more deeply into the world around him than just following an ordinary life. That was interesting.

Q: Did you have personal contact with Mr. Hoover?

Admiral Keith: Yes. On the return trip, all the young ensigns were invited up to tea with Mrs. Hoover, and all the senior officers had dinner in the cabin in turn, rotation, with the President and Mrs. Hoover.

---

* Herbert C. Hoover, who served as President of the United States from March 1929 to March 1933, was elected in November 1928.
† "Different ships, different long splices" is a traditional Navy saying that means the same as the popular, "Different strokes for different folks."

One thing that is an interesting piece of history, I think, is that the ensigns on board the Utah had a game they called medicine ball.[*]

I'm sure many people on carriers and battleships--any ship where there's room enough--played bull-in-the ring with a medicine ball. Mr. Hoover saw that, and he got a medicine ball from us, and he started in playing before breakfast in the morning with the Wilbur brothers, with Mr. Hurley, with some of the newspapermen.[†] He had Arthur Krock on board, he had Mark Sullivan on board, he had a man whose name, I believe, was Smith, who had a graduate brother in 1925, who was from Buffalo, New York. His name I'm not too sure of. But they were distinguished people in the newspaper world, writers who were on the Utah. They all joined in the medicine ball game. When Mr. Hoover became President, he had a medicine ball cabinet that met with him for breakfast and played medicine ball with him at the White House. They consisted of some members of Congress and some members of his Cabinet. So the Utah had an influence on Mr. Hoover.

Shortly after that cruise and shortly after Mr. Hoover became President, the Navy put Russell Train in as his naval White House aide.[‡] He took a laundry room in the basement of the White House, and instead of having dealings in Iran, he did a great deal of good for the Navy in establishing a firm position which lasted through the assignment of very able captains to the White House as presidential aides, through until Eisenhower became President.[§]

President Eisenhower did not want a senior officer as an aide; he wanted a young man.[**] He required that the Navy send him lieutenant commanders or commanders--I've forgotten which--and the same for the Army. They downgraded the ranks of the aides, and

---

[*] A medicine ball is a leather-covered ball, about the same size as a basketball but considerably heavier. Individuals toss it back and forth in conditioning exercises.
[†] Curtis D. Wilbur was the Secretary of the Navy at the time; his brother, Ray Lyman Lyman Wilbur became Secretary of the Interior in the Hoover administration; Patrick J. Hurley became Secretary of War in 1929.
[‡] Captain Train served as naval aide to the President from June 1930 to May 1932.
[§] This is a reference to Vice Admiral John Poindexter, USN, who was President Ronald Reagan's national security adviser in the mid-1980s. He was involved in the controversial Iran-Contra arms deals that were prominent in the news at the time of this interview.
[**] Dwight D. Eisenhower served as President of the United States from January 1953 to January 1961.

with that downgrading, we lost a very happy position for the Navy in the White House. Those aides that served during the period that I spoke of first were liked by their boss and had an opportunity to see the boss and to talk to the boss, so that there was a naval voice in the White House that had an opportunity to say some of the things that the Navy wanted to get said in the proper ear. The Navy was sad when Eisenhower made his decision.

Q: Admiral Davidson told me that he had been recommended for that job when Eisenhower became President, but, as you say, the new President wanted to downgrade it, so Eisenhower got Commander Ned Beach instead.[*]

Admiral Keith: Well, after Mr. Hoover arrived, we left Rio Christmas night, 1928.[†] As we steamed out of the harbor, a full moon was over the Sugarloaf Mountain, one of the most beautiful scenes I've ever seen in my life. From every hilltop surrounding Rio, fireworks were flying. So at the end of the cruise, it seemed to us, that the President-elect had succeeded in his desire to establish some goodwill with our neighbors to the south.

Q: You were fortunate in that not all of your junior officer shipmates were able to make that cruise, were they?

Admiral Keith: No. There were 36 ensigns on board the Utah in those days, packed away three to a room, and in gun rooms.

I don't know whether you'll want to leave this in the history or not, but as an aside, one of the 5-inch gun rooms on the Utah/Florida class was made into a bunkroom with eight bunks in it. When they put the gun ports in and went to sea, eight young human beings were shut up in there for a couple of weeks. It made things a little funky. It was the

---

[*] Commander/Captain Edward L. Beach, USN, served as naval aide to the President from January 1953 to February 1957. The Naval Institute oral history of Rear Admiral John F. Davidson, USN (Ret.), covers the desire to lower the seniority of the aide from that of his predecessors. President Harry Truman's last naval aide was Rear Admiral Robert L. Dennison, USN, Naval Academy class of 1923. Beach, his relief, was in the class of 1939.

[†] Mr. and Mrs. Hoover boarded the ship 18 December at Montevideo, Urugay. The ship then went to Rio de Janeiro, Brazil.

duty--or unfortunate assignment, let us say--of one of those ensigns to stand captain's inspection as the ensign in charge, to receive the comments that fell upon that unlucky individual.

Over on the Florida, there was a famous story from Red Christie, who was a very quick man with a word.* He didn't like the smell of this station which he had to man, so he sprayed it heavily with foo-foo. When the captain arrived, he took a couple of sniffs, and he said, "Smells like a two-bit whorehouse, doesn't it, Mr. Christie?"

Mr. Christie immediately answered, "I don't know, Captain. I've never been in one." [Laughter] That ended the inspection on the Florida for that day. But that is beside the point.

We were leaving Rio in a beautiful setting, and the gun ports were not in. We had two movies going, one forward and one aft, and we sat in reclining deck chairs to watch them. The Utah was pretty well equipped for this cruise. Besides all the gunnery exercises and all those drills, you read a lot, you played deck tennis, you did all sorts of things.

On Christmas night, once we'd cleared the harbor, we were cruising in the tropics. The table was set on deck for Christmas dinner for all the officers and all the newspapermen and all of Mr. Hoover's guests. Well, I had heard Mr. Hoover speak on occasion in various cities, and he was not a dynamic speaker. He was not a very interesting speaker, and he didn't come across very well.

That evening he got up and addressed himself to the press and presented his thoughts about the position of the press in his political world and in the well-being of the United States. He was an enthusiastic speaker; he was alive; he came across with great vigor. It was a transformation that, for a young ensign, was absolutely astounding. And it did one more thing for me, as a young man. It made me realize just how much the politician is dependent upon his press and how interested he was in having a favorable one. I don't remember what he said, but the manner in which he delivered that speech was very, very impressive. It was also astonishing that a change in subject could change a man's whole attitude and his whole physiognomy almost, in the way he looked and the way he spoke.

---

* Ensign Carl G. Christie, USN.

Q: Was there a Secret Service detail along with the President?

Q: Well, we took one down with us, and he got on the first boat up to Buenos Aires, after we got into Montevideo. He sent a secret wire back to the ship, asking us, please, to go to his stateroom and get his pistol; he had forgotten it. [Laughter] So that led to a few comments around the officer corps of the Navy about the Secret Service guarding the President.

Q: What do you remember about the junior officer mess in that ship?

Admiral Keith: Nothing that I can record for history. [Laughter]

We went from the presidential cruise to a fleet exercise which we joined in progress in the Panama area.* We transited the canal and went over to join the force protecting the canal from a raid by the carrier Saratoga. At dawn one morning I was on watch in turret number one, and through my periscope I saw the launching of an attack. The Utah hadn't gotten lost during the night. We were with the enemy. But I saw a dawn launch of planes from a carrier for the first time in my life, and this was a tremendously impressive sight. They were silhouetted against the light of the rising sun, which wasn't yet over the horizon. You had a realization right then as to what a weapon that was then and would be in the future.

In Guantanamo, at the end of the fleet problem, I don't know why, but here I was--not a year out of the Naval Academy--and I went to a fleet problem critique for the first time. I heard all the officers who had the planning, the detailing, the tactical arrangements, get up and talk. This added to my knowledge of the Navy, my interest in what was going on around me. I was no longer thinking about just manning a turret and getting some powder and bullets up. Now I was able to look at what part the Navy was playing, to begin

---

* Fleet Problem IX, which took place 23-27 January 1929, marked the first time the new aircraft carriers Lexington (CV-2) and Saratoga (CV-3) participated in a fleet problem. The Saratoga's planes made a successful attack on the Panama Canal. For an excellent account, see Eugene E. Wilson, "The Navy's First Carrier Task Force," U.S. Naval Institute Proceedings, February 1950, pages 158-169.

to look towards what was going on in the world. I never missed another fleet problem critique after that. I had that kind of interest right from the beginning.

That first fleet problem gave me a much broader picture of the Navy and what the strategy was. Codebreaking came into my ken for the first time, when I went and heard people talk about what they'd learned from the little bit of code that they broke. I knew that they'd taken a lieutenant off of our ship, sent him to the flag staff to work in codes.

Q: Do you remember who that was?

Admiral Keith: No, I don't. He was the third division officer on the USS Utah in 1928, but I don't know his name.

*　　　*　　　*

In the summer of 1929 the Utah went into Kiel, Germany, where I had as proud a moment as I think I've ever had in the United States Navy. We saw German youth on parade. We saw girls that looked like Amazons out on the water in eight-oared shells. Just about every youth we saw was big, vigorous, and looked like a million dollars. They really were wonderful-looking young kids. I was seeing this country for my first time, and as I wandered around the streets of Kiel, I was just impressed at what the German people were really like.

Then I saw a young American fire controlman who was on shore patrol duty. He had his hat squared away on his head, he stood about six feet, he was solidly made, his uniform was spotlessly white. He was walking his beat down the street, with his billy just swinging like this. He had a nice way of handling it as he'd swing it around. I said, "Boy, they breed 'em pretty damn good in America, too, you know." He just made you proud to be an American.

That same cruise, we went to Paris, and when I went into a dining room, I heard some American and his wife having breakfast. They called over the waiter, and in a loud voice, they put on a sad performance of browbeating a poor servant in the hotel because they were paying the bill. It made you ashamed to be an American.

So you have a growing-up experience. This was in '29, when I was 24 years old, and I had both of those experiences. Eight years later, I was in charge of shore patrol; 11

years later, on another shore patrol, I was told a sailor was hiding under a madam's bed. So you get this, you get that, and you put it all together, and you come to what you call growing up.

Q: What are your recollections of standing deck watches in the Utah?

Admiral Keith: Well, I recollect standing watch with the senior watch officer, Doggy Newell, who was breaking me in.* On midwatches we would talk, and I thought he was crazy.† He started talking about sitting down and figuring out the positions of stars at certain times and putting it all on tables, so you could go into the tables and not have to work each star individually, but it was all done for you ahead of time.‡ I knew there would be a lot of manpower involved in doing this, because it would all have to be done with nothing better than an adding machine in those days, but working out a Marcq St.-Hilaire.§ For every star that you worked, you worked a sheet of paper that was about 11 or 12 inches long, the size of a pad today.

Lo and behold, when we came to make-work programs under Mr. Roosevelt in 1934, he found a lot of mathematicians out of work, and we came up with a new navigation system.** Here was what this man Newell had been talking about.

I stood watches with another man, Jerry Doolin, who married an Annapolis girl, and he knew the heavens from one end to the other.†† I was just amazed at how he could pick out the stars and say this, that, this. Although I've navigated by the stars a good many times myself, I never had his facility or ability to identify the stars in the heavens. Certain planets,

---

* Lieutenant Edward L. Newell, USN.
† On board Navy ships, the midwatch runs from 2345 at night to 0345 in the morning.
‡ This is a description of the calculations involved in fixing the ship's position by celestial navigation.
§ In 1875 a man named Marcq St.-Hilaire worked out a celestial navigation technique known as the altitude intercept method.
** Franklin D. Roosevelt was President of the United States from March 1933 to April 1945. The Hydrographic Office publications involving short methods were H.O. 208 and H.O. 211.
†† Lieutenant Edward H. Doolin, USN.

certain stars I know barely, but he was friends with all of them. So these are things you remember about your early days.

I think we've covered my awakening in the Utah. Going from when I was a midshipman and a fresh-caught ensign, I knew really nothing about the Navy. Sure, I'd had four years of exposure to education and been on summer cruises, and it was all enlightening. But really to know what life in the fleet was like, you began to find out when you got on board ship.

I also began to know something of the correlation between politics and the press. Mr. Hoover's goodwill tour to South America began showing me that our President was looking at world affairs, as well as being President of the United States. This is something I probably realized, but the first time I ever had it really demonstrated to me was then, and I put that away in the back of my mind.

I don't think any young man really knows what he wants to do in life until he gets out and gains some experience. We had a two-year obligation when we graduated in 1928. By the time I ended my two years, whether I wanted to be a naval officer, or whether I didn't, there wasn't any job on the outside. In two years it was 1930; the Depression had started.[*] We had had a pay cut, but we were getting paid regularly. We were lucky people; we were rich people. Rich ensigns, they used to call us.

Q: Your time in that ship ended in 1930. What was the reason for a number of officers transferring from the Utah to the Arizona?

Admiral Keith: Utah went out of commission and did not recommission until they made her a target ship and refitted her, taking a lot of guns off and everything.[†] She was a target ship with great pieces of timber, so that they could actually bomb and then have her live to be bombed again.

---

[*] Following the crash of the New York Stock Exchange in late October 1929, the United States was plunged into the Great Depression, from which it did not recover until the nation geared up for World War II at the beginning of the 1940s. The Depression was marked by high unemployment and many business failures.

[†] In 1931-32 the Utah was converted to a mobile target ship. On 1 July 1931 her hull number changed to AG-16. She was recommissioned 1 April 1932.

Q: She was demilitarized as the result of the disarmament treaty.

Admiral Keith: I guess so. I don't know whether they took her turrets off or not. She's a hulk out in Pearl Harbor, and I never looked to see. I don't remember, although I've been out there.*

Q: You said earlier that the Utah had the bad reputation on the East Coast and the Arizona on the West. Did you find that to be true when you got to the Arizona?†

Admiral Keith: When I went to the Arizona, Mr. Hoover wanted to take another cruise. So he picked out what was then known as the poorhouse of the Caribbean and went to Puerto Rico. The idea was that he could learn more about their problems, and he hoped to find some way to do something about it. At least that's the way it seemed to us. We went into Ponce, and we cruised home from there.‡ He went across country to San Juan and saw the countryside and came back, sailed a week later. He had some of his Cabinet on board. I can remember Wilbur and Hurley being there and one tall, lean man whose name I can't remember anymore.

Q: Did you have any encounters with Commander Thomson?§

---

* A photo of the Utah, taken in 1941, appears on page 52 of the December 1976 issue of the U.S. Naval Institute Proceedings. It shows that three turrets had been removed; two turrets without guns remained.
† The USS Arizona (BB-39) was commissioned 17 October 1916. Following modernization at the Norfolk Navy Yard from 1929 to 1931 she had a standard displacement of 34,200 tons, was 608 feet long and 106 feet in the beam. Her top speed was 21.2 knots. She was armed with 12 14-inch guns and 12 5-inch/51 broadside guns, and eight 5-inch/25 antiaircraft guns.
‡ Hoover was on board the Arizona 19-29 March 1931. The ship anchored at Ponce, Puerto Rico, 23-24 March, and at St. Thomas, Virgin Islands, 25 March. See Paul Stillwell, Battleship Arizona: An Illustrated History (Annapolis: Naval Institute Press, 1991), pages 112-120.
§ Commander Thaddeus A. Thomson, Jr., USN, was temporary commanding officer of the Arizona from 29 April 1930 to 20 September 1930, at which time he became executive officer.

Admiral Keith: Who talked about him, John Davidson?[*]

Q: Yes, he did.

Admiral Keith: [Laughter]

Q: He didn't speak very favorably of him, either.

Admiral Keith: John was his executive assistant. He had to sit in the office with him all day. Commander Thomson was a browbeater. He would love to get somebody that he could just belabor with words, and he would let them have it.

I took over six ensigns with me, as the senior one from the Utah, the Utah going out of commission, the Arizona going in. I reported to Commander Thomson, and I reported with a draft of six ensigns. He said, "Keith? Keith? Oh, I remember you. I remember you very well."

When he was exec of Bancroft Hall, I played on the baseball team at Annapolis.[†] He had to let you realize that you were getting a privilege to be excused from serving extra duty for your demerits because you were on an athletic squad on a Wednesday and Saturday. You had to go up personally and stand outside his door until he was ready to see you. You'd go in and report that you had demerits for such and such. So I must have had enough of them to make my visits ones that he would remember. So he said he remembered me.

I took over the after two turrets, and Stuart Smith in '25 took over the two forward turrets, we being experienced turret officers.[‡] We had the whole division. We were six months from commissioning, and we were beginning to assemble our crew. We had so

---

[*] Ensign John F. Davidson, USN, was one of the junior officers who transferred with Keith from the Utah to the Arizona.
[†] Bancroft Hall is the large multi-wing dormitory that houses Naval Academy midshipmen. It also contains the offices of members of the executive department, including the commandant, executive officer, and battalion and company officers.
[‡] Lieutenant (junior grade) James Stuart Smith, Jr., USN, Naval Academy class of 1925.

many men each assigned to those two turrets on the <u>Arizona</u>--divisions one and two, three and four.*

We were required to make out and present to the executive officer on Saturday a work list for the next week of what we intended to do. I had sent mine in to the exec's office on Saturday morning and was in civilian clothes at quarter to 1:00, ready to leave the ship. I got a knock on the door, and there was the exec's orderly. He wanted to see me. So I got in uniform, went back to see Thad. He said he had my work list, and he didn't understand why I had only two men available to do work for the first lieutenant and the supply officer in preparing their storerooms, which they had no men assigned to. I said, "Sir, may I go and get my list? I'll answer your question as best I can."

He said, "Certainly."

So I went back to my stateroom, checked my list, brought it back with me. I said, "Sir, here these jobs are assigned, the man-hours. Every one of them is completely assigned to work that I think is necessary in my part of the ship."

He said, "Yes, but Lieutenant Smith, in the forward part, has the same number of men you do. You have two men available to work for the supply department, and he has 18."

I said, "Can I see his list?" Then I said, "He just hasn't got as much to do forward as I have back here, sir. I've got the catapults to get ready, and I'm working on this, that, and the other."

Well, we argued from 1:00 o'clock until 5:00. I would go back, sit down, check my figures, go back and talk to him. Finally, he said, "Mr. Keith, I enunciated the policy of making as many men available to work for the first lieutenant and supply, who have no men, as possible from your and Smith's division. You have not carried out those instructions."

I said, "Sir, they must have been issued before I came on board, because your policy and my policy, sir, are just 180 degrees out of phase. My policy is to get everything done in my part of the ship, and if there's anything left over for them, that's what I'm going to give

---

* Eventually, each turret would have its own division officer; during the modernization Keith and Smith each had half the main battery.

them. If you had told me your policy at 1:00 o'clock, we'd both have been ashore along time ago." [Laughter]

He laughed, and I said, "I really didn't see that order. That must have come out before I came on board. It wasn't in my files. I've never seen that one. Let me go over this list again." So I went back, came in, and gave him 16 men. But from that time on, because I had stood up and argued with him, I never was asked to take his browbeating. But I have been called into his cabin when he had his chief yeoman sitting there, taking dictation, and he would call in a lieutenant, who was senior to me but was assistant to the first lieutenant. He would just belabor him in front of the chief and in front of me, his junior, give him all sorts of hell. You could see that man stand there with his hands behind his back, with his hands clenched till they were white, he was so damn mad. He was ready to kill that guy! But this is the kind of person that John Davidson described to you.

Q: Do you have any recollections of the trip from the Atlantic to the Pacific in the Arizona when she was going around to rejoin the fleet?

Admiral Keith: Nothing particular, no. Always it was an experience to go through the Gulf of Tehuantepec. You hit some pretty rough seas in there.

Q: How well did she ride in a heavy sea?

Admiral Keith: Well, compared to riding a destroyer, it's a pretty simple proposition. In a hurricane in the Caribbean, those four-pipers can pretty well stand on end.

Q: What do you recall about steaming in formation with other ships?

Admiral Keith: I recall always being on the bridge, which a junior officer was required to be whenever there were maneuvers. I recall being told by my seniors what your rights were as officer of the deck. I remember what your responsibilities were as officer of the deck.

You were given a pretty good course of sprouts as a junior officer.*

I remember a time in the Arizona that we were maneuvering after we reached the Pacific. I was the officer of the deck, and I had the conn.† Then Captain Freeman gave an order to the wheel.‡ I took my glasses off, went over, and hung them up. He said, "What's the matter?"

I said, "I recognize that you can assume the conn anytime you want. When you gave an order, I assumed you had, sir."

Q: A little bit impertinent on your part.

Admiral Keith: No. I was standing up for my rights. He made me his representative, and this was one of the things they told you young. On the Utah, at least, they had said, "The exec and the captain can assume the conn from you--nobody else." (I may be mistaken; maybe the navigator can.) They told me, "No one, when you have the deck, can give an order to the wheel as a representative of the captain unless they have relieved you. And you'd better protect your right." I think I gained respect from Captain Freeman. I know that he and I got along very well. We had our differences, but he recognized that I had a right to be heard, and he listened to me. If he found fault, I had a right to defend myself, and I did.

Q: Some years earlier there had been a turret explosion in the Mississippi.§ Did that govern some of your safety procedures in the Arizona?

---

* "Course of sprouts" essentially refers to on-the-job training.
† The individual with the conn--normally an officer--directs the ship's movements in course and speed.
‡ Captain Charles S. Freeman, USN, commanded the USS Arizona (BB-39) from 20 September 1930 to 20 June 1932.
§ While the USS Mississippi (BB-41) was engaged in gunnery practice on 12 June 1924, turret two exploded, killing 48 men and injuring 9.

Admiral Keith: There had been one there and one on the Colorado. A gun blew up on the Colorado when I was in the Arizona. She had an explosion during a night gun fire.[*]

Yes, naturally, any accident is investigated, and Navy safety precautions--unfortunately, for too many times--were written only after an accident brought an incorrect procedure to your attention. The Arizona's turrets each had three guns in a single slide, and you had to load four bags of powder from the carts coming up on the side, then pass them across this tray and this tray, to the center tray. Then you loaded two of them by hand and rammed the other one with the rammer, the last two, and pushed them all the way in.

I can remember that we went over to observe another battleship that had put an E on the turret for the last two years, and they felt sure that they were going to be able to put an E on the turret again.[†] I had observed this ship, as a safety observer, when they had a casualty in handling ammunition. You could just see that their first thought was, "There goes our E," and with an E went an extra $10.00 or $15.00 a month for every man that was in that turret. So rather than handling the casualty, you could see that there was a sense of loss, of desperation, or what the hell. They didn't handle the casualty well, and they didn't get off any more shots.

So I talked to my gunnery officer on the Arizona about this, and I said, "I've been a turret officer in the Utah, and the reports that I'm sending to you on my check sight, how many hits we get, if I check sight six hits in six shots, I take one or two of them off and report they weren't on target when they pressed the key." I said, "I'm convinced that if you get a crew thinking from the check sight records that they're hot, and that they're going to get an E, then if something goes wrong, they are going to go phlooey and not think and not carry out their recovery procedures or the proper procedures. So this is the way I'm running things."

---

[*] The incident Admiral Keith referred to was probably a plotting room fire, not turret explosion, that took place on board the USS Colorado (BB-45) on 3 June 1930. To extinguish the fire, the crew flooded the plotting room and adjacent areas, resulting in $200,000 in damage.

[†] An "E," for excellence, is generally awarded to a ship or component of a ship as a result of top performance in competition with other ships during a given time period.

Well, interestingly enough, every night on the screens at the movie Captain Freeman saw that the Keith turret was last in the check sight. This was every single night--never first, never second, always last. Maybe I was overdoing it, but I had a casualty.

One time two strong-armed boys--from Missouri, let's say, good country lads--rammed the powder bags too far into the center gun. The powder bags for short-range battle practice weighed 10, 20, or 30 pounds less than the service charges. I think it was 90 pounds against 120 pounds for the regular bags. They were so used to pushing those drill bags in that when they got 90-pound bags, they almost threw them out of the muzzle. At any rate, the bag was so far in that the primer didn't fire the black powder charge in the rear of the bag, and I got a report, "Hang fire in center gun."

The chief turret captain had already given the order to elevate the guns. We elevated to the magnificent number of degrees that they built into the Arizona on modernization.* They came back down, reprimed, picked up the target--BANGO!--off went the projectile. Even with an alleged hang fire, we finished first. The second set got all hits. It was a rough day, and we got hits on the first shot. The one that we fired after the hang fire didn't hit, but the next set of pointers came in, and they did very well.† The gunnery officer was on his way up to see me when I came out of the turret after the practice, and he said, "You didn't check your primers."

I said, "How's that?"

He said, "Well, you had a hang fire, and we knew we had some bad primers in this lot. You were supposed to check them all, to see whether the cap was right and whatever tests we could make on them."

I said, "Oh, no, sir. My chief turret captain got the primer out. Here it is; it fired. We had a hang fire because we threw the short-range battle practice bags too far into the gun, and we had to elevate and handle the hang fire to get them back down where the flame

---

* The range of the Arizona's 14-inch guns was increased during the modernization when their maximum elevation was increased from 15 degrees to 30 degrees.
† Pointers and trainers were the terms used for the individuals who aimed the guns in elevation and azimuth.

could reach them." So that was the end of that. That isn't what you were asking me, but that's an example of a difference in approach to the way you train.

Q: Do you have any comparisons of the Atlantic and Pacific fleets in that era?

Admiral Keith: In the Utah we'd gone from our home yard to Guantanamo as a training cycle, gunnery training, and spent some port visits in New England on midshipman cruises in the summertime. That was the Atlantic program. We weren't a year-around fleet. We went into the yard around the end of November, started the fleet problem early in January, which was always the month where all ships were in their home ports or their home yards. Same way on the Pacific Coast, with a different schedule. Those ships all went up and made fleet week in Seattle, fleet week in Portland, Oregon, fleet week in San Francisco in the summertime. Then they came back and made serious endeavors in going through the gunnery training schedules. They usually had a fleet problem that came in, where the Atlantic and Pacific fleets got together again. Again, each one of those, when they had a critique, Ensign Keith was there and began to learn a little bit more. It added to my interest in what was going on in the Navy.

*   *   *

From the Arizona, I went to the Overton.* I don't know how many times you've heard this, but you were told, when you got into destroyers, the 1,200-ton four-pipers, "You're now getting in the real Navy. You'll walk down the deck in the morning, and a man will see you and salute you and say, 'Good morning, sir.' In time, you'll walk down the deck, and the men will salute you and say, 'Good morning, Mr. Keith.' In time, you'll walk down the deck, and they'll say, 'Good morning, Mr. Keith,' and you can say, 'Good morning, Johnson. Good morning, Williams,' whatever the name is. Gradually you'll come to know the members of your crew. Then you're a shipmate."

---

* USS Overton (DD-239), a Clemson-class destroyer, was commissioned 30 June 1920. Standard displacement was 1,190 tons, length 314 feet, and beam of 32 feet. Top speed was 35 knots. She was armed with four 4-inch guns, one 3-inch gun, and 12 21-inch torpedo tubes.

People told you, "The most important thing that you must learn is to know people in the other ships that are nested with you, because in keeping station at 200 yards, when you can recognize people sitting on the john in the destroyer ahead of you, you know you're too damn close; take some turns off." [Laughter] So, history or no history, these are things you can't help but remember when you get to talking.

* * *

The Overton went to Panama as part of the Special Service Squadron, and we were very undermanned. I had 11 sailor men in the deck force. I had assigned to the ship 45 Marines, who were supposed to swab the decks and keep it clean and man the boats and do all the things that seamen do.

Unfortunately for the cleanliness and care of the Overton, the Marines were put ashore in Nicaragua, and we saw them very rarely during our two years in Panama, from 1932 to '34. But we did go up and down both coasts. We went through the canal to Bluefields, and we went to Puerto Cabezas.[*] I saw and came to know a good many Nicaraguans in the capital city. The memory that I have of them is that they were genial. There were many people who wanted to have a government that they had a voice in, that finally the revolutionary Sandino acceded to an election to be held under the supervision of the Marines.[†] These Marines were stationed in every village and hamlet of the country of Nicaragua, and they supervised the election. That's when the Somoza family came into power, and they lasted until just here recently, when they were ousted.[‡] So we established not a republic, but we established another dynasty.

I saw some really poor people in Nicaragua. But there were many of them who were glad the Marines were in there, and glad they had a chance to go to the polls and vote.

---

[*] Both of these ports are on the eastern, Caribbean Sea, side of the country.
[†] U.S. Marines were in Nicaragua almost continuously from 1912 to 1933. They were subject to raids by a rebel leader, General Augusto César Sandino, from whom the Sandinistas took their name. He was murdered by national guardsmen in 1934.
[‡] In 1937, General Anastasio Somoza, head of the National Guard, became President. His family ruled Nicaragua until 1979, when his son, Major General Anastasio Somoza Debayle was ousted by Sandinista guerrillas. Sandinista rule ended in 1990 with the election of Violetta Chamorro as President.

This was something that you had to realize, that it takes all kinds of people to make up the world, and that we have some responsibility to try to give those who choose to be free a chance to be.

When we left, we took the Marines out from Puerto Cabezas on January 1, 1933. If you ever saw a New Year's Eve hoedown, it was when the Marines were going to march on board the <u>Overton</u>. We went out of there with our gunwales practically awash because of all the stuff that they brought on board and all the people that they brought on board. We took them back to Panama, and that was practically the end of our requirement for being down there. But we did see a good deal of Marines. We saw enough of the people of Nicaragua to feel that there must be a carryover today from people of goodwill in that country that we saw down there 50 years ago.

So there are things that you can go back to and say that whether you are on the right side or the wrong side, there is a right side down there, from my experience, and you can hope that the Contras are the right people to be backing.[*] There are experiences that you've had along the way that lead you to wonder how these judgments should be made.

In the days that I'm talking about, 1933, a flight from Norfolk to Panama by our flying boats of that period was an event. Usually they flew nonstop to Honduras and then flew on to Panama after refueling. The first nonstop flight was scheduled for September of 1933. The <u>Overton</u>'s tour was finished, and we were heading back for Norfolk, so we were sent to Cayman Islands to anchor and stand by until the flight took off from Norfolk. The <u>Overton</u> was to be a rescue and beacon ship.

Before the weather was satisfactory for the flight to start, the Sergeants' Revolution took place in Cuba.[†] The <u>Overton</u> was ordered to proceed to the Isle of Pines, where the state prison was located. The captain and the chief engineer of our ship, along with the doctor and the paymaster, went ashore about 9:00 o'clock. One of the things they were

---

[*] At the time of this interview, the United States was supplying aid to the Nicaraguan Contras in their struggle against the Sandinistas that had ousted the Somoza regime.
[†] In August 1933, Cuban President Gerardo Machado left the country as a result of a revolution led by Fulgencio Batista, a sergeant in the Cuban Army. Batista also became a dictator and remained in power until ousted by Fidel Castro on New Year's Day in 1959.

supposed to do was find out as to the safety of 75 Cuban officers, Army and Navy, who had been captured or taken by the sergeants and incarcerated in this federal prison. They'd been brought out from Cienfuegos. We made our report, and the report said that there were only 73 officers there. On board the Richmond, which was the flagship of Admiral Freeman, he had Pedro del Valle.* I don't know whether you've ever gotten any oral history from him.

Q: He wrote his own book.†

Admiral Keith: He did? He was the Marine officer on the staff of ComSpeRon, the Special Service Squadron. Admiral Freeman also had Roscoe Hillenkoetter, who just died recently.‡

Q: Was this the Freeman who had been your skipper in the Arizona?

Admiral Keith: Freeman had been my skipper in the Arizona. So they had gotten into Havana, and they'd established contact with Batista. When they got this report, del Valle went over to see Batista and said, "Look, you're not giving us the straight dope. You told us you had 75 officers in this state prison, and there are only 73 there."

Batista said, "I was given the information there were 75. I'll find out." So he came back and said, "There was an old Cuban who had taken sick as they were leaving Cienfuegos, and his son was also an officer, a young man. We sent the son ashore with the father, and the father was in the hospital. The son sees him every day.

"Okay," said Pedro.

---

* Rear Admiral Charles S. Freeman, USN, Commander Special Service Squadron. Major Pedro A. del Valle, USMC.
† In addition to his oral history with the Marine Corps Historical Center, Lieutenant General Pedro A. del Valle, USMC (Ret.), wrote Semper Fidelis: An Autobiography (Hawthorne, California: Christian Book Club of America, 1976). It contains a section about the author's experiences in the Caribbean while on board the Richmond.
‡ Lieutenant Roscoe H. Hillenkoetter, USN, was Admiral Freeman's aide and flag secretary. Hillenkoetter died 18 June 1982.

I was in Havana later on in the Overton. We dragged anchor while we rode out a West Indian hurricane in Havana Harbor. We dragged until we finally were able to hook onto a pier and tie up, and the Cuban guards on the pier said, "You can't do this."

We had more guns than they did, and we said, "We think we will--till the storm's over, anyhow." [Laughter]

I was on board the Richmond, watching a movie one night, and a note was delivered to Pedro del Valle, who was a friend of mine. He scribbled something on it and sent it back. I said, "What was that?"

He said, "It's a note from Batista. They're going to raid the Communist headquarters at 9:30 tonight, and I told him I want to see the end of this movie. I told him I couldn't get there till 10:15, to hold up." [Laughter]

These three--Captain Creesy, who ended up in the Marine quartermaster corps and was quartermaster general at one time; del Valle; and Roscoe Hillenkoetter--were all completely fluent in Spanish.[*] They were ashore every night, and they established quite a rapport with Batista. The only guidance that they had was through the Navy Department down there, because Sumner Welles wanted his man, who, if my memory serves me, was Grau San Martin, to be President.[†] The sergeants had come along, and he was not made the president.[‡]

So our ambassador was not doing very much in trying to find out what was going on in Havana, and these people were finding out a great deal and feeding it into Washington. We had by this time closed the Postgraduate School, and all the officers there had gone off to Philadelphia and manned the out-of-commission destroyers up there. They had gotten crews for them, and they had enough destroyers manned to bring Cuba around with destroyers in the various ports, to protect Americans from incursions of any kind or to protect American interests.

---

[*] Captain Andrew E. Creesy, USMC, commanded the Marine detachment in the flagship Richmond (CL-9).
[†] Sumner Welles was U.S. ambassador to Cuba from April through December 1933. He later served as Under Secretary of State from 1937 to 1943.
[‡] Ramon Grau San Martin served as President for four months shortly after the revolution but was soon replaced by a candidate put forth by Batista's junta.

My skipper, Bill Forrestel, was well-known to Admiral Freeman, and he was sent around to pick up information and make personal reports, when he got back to Panama, about how things were going.* We went into one of the little harbors on the north coast of Cuba; there aren't very many of them. The J. Fred Talbott was in there, and she was the ship that relieved us. They transferred a classmate of mine, Bob Morris, over to the J. Fred Talbott, along with our Marine detachment, our doctor, and our paymaster.† They were supposed to be in that port, as I say, to look after American interests, but they had specific orders not to go ashore at night, not to land any troops.

Bob Morris came on board the Overton to see me, and he said, "I'm in trouble. My skipper and the exec and the chief engineer are going into the skipper's cabin every morning after breakfast and start drinking rum. They help raids ashore with armed troops, they go ashore and stay after sunset." He said, "Actually, the ship is not ready to perform its duties under the leadership that's there." He said, "If I had anybody else on board to back me, I think I ought to take command of the ship and put them under arrest. So what am I going to do?"

So I said, "I'll be in Havana tonight and tomorrow morning. Hang on. I'll see if I can do anything."

So I went over to see my friend Hillenkoetter. I said, "Hilly, what do you think of my judgment?" Here I was, a big shining junior lieutenant then.

He said, "I like it."

I said, "If I told you that you ought to get the J. Fred Talbott in here and take a look at what's going on on there, and didn't give you any other reasons than that, what would you do?"

He said, "I'd think about it." He apparently went and saw the admiral, because J. Fred Talbott was ordered to proceed immediately to Havana. She came in just before sunset. The captain, chief engineer, and exec all went ashore. They went to the Nacional Hotel, went in the dining room, and they were having dinner there after sunset. Sumner

---

* Lieutenant Commander William J. Forrestel, USN.
† Lieutenant (junior grade) Robert L. Morris, USN.

Welles came in to have dinner with some Cubans. Sumner Welles wasn't too popular, I guess, with the Navy. They made remarks that he objected to. He went back to his office and sent a message to the admiral, reported that three of his officers were insulting, or whatever you want to say. I don't know what was in the message, but I know that we received a message to provide two officers to be a part of an inspection that was ordered for 7:00 o'clock the next morning. I went over, and Bob told me they had the captain in the shower for two hours, under cold water, trying to get him in shape. I went down.

[Interruption]*

The United States had a magnificent opportunity, as I saw it from my position in Cuba in 1933, to guide Batista in his establishment of his reign in Cuba. They flunked the test. He went on to become a dictator. He abused his position to feather his nest financially. He took care of his cronies; he didn't take care of his people. But it seems to me that a man whom I know said Batista's position as an ex-sergeant in 1933 was, "Tell me what I should do, and I'll do it."

For us not to have some capability, if we believe in our democracy, to help a man who wants help to establish one, and to make him believe in it, then there's something wrong with the way we're doing business.

Q: It could be, though, that his attitude changed over time, and he got arrogant and decided he didn't need that help anymore.

Admiral Keith: Okay. But we still flunked, if we had the opportunity, when he said: "Tell me what I should do, and I'll do it."

*   *   *

---

* Unfortunately, after the interruption Admiral Keith did not tell what became of the three officers from the J. Fred Talbott.

In your first destroyer days, you really learned that money is what pays for the number of men that the Navy has. We had much less than our assigned allowance of personnel to man the ship in peacetime. Since the ships weren't fully manned, you had to improvise and learn how to live with the situation that you were in. To save money we had reduced charges of ammunition for all of our practices in those days.

The money for overhauls was drastically reduced. It changed from a relatively short period between overhauls to a longer one. In the Destroyer Force Atlantic, they established what was known as a rotating reserve, and the overhaul of those ships was accomplished as the various yards up and down the coast had a chance to work the destroyers' maintenance and repairs in around the overhauls of the larger and more important ships of the fleet. So a destroyer overhaul, which for a four-piper probably took two months, would be extended to anywhere from six to eight, ten months. The Overton spent from the fall of 1933 till the spring of 1934 getting an overhaul in Norfolk Navy Yard.

I found out the shipyard didn't always know what they had. I needed to find out whether my guns needed to be relined. They said they didn't have a star gauge, so that they couldn't run it through and see what the actual bore diameters of the guns were. I went around and found an old chief who had been in the Navy a long time, and he said, "Sure, there's one up in such and such a building in the attic." So they went and found it, and I star-gauged my guns. But all this was a growing experience; all this was something you add to your knowledge.

*   *   *

Then I went to the Nitro, carrying ammunition.* I saw more ports than I've seen in all the years since in the Navy.

Q: Where did you operate in that ship?

---

* The USS Nitro (AE-2) was commissioned 1 April 1921. She was 483 feet long, 61 feet in the beam, had a draft of 21 feet, and displaced 10,600 tons. She had a top speed of 13 knots. She was armed with four 5-inch guns and two 3-inch antiaircraft guns.

Admiral Keith: We went from Boston to Seattle, and we touched base practically everywhere, even up at Iona Island, the ammunition depot there up the Hudson River. We steamed up the Hudson River under the bridges in the Nitro, went into Newport, went into New London, to Yorktown, Norfolk. You name it, we went.

One very interesting thing about the Nitro was our trip to Wake Island. We arrived with a load of ammunition for West Loch in Pearl Harbor. While there, we were told we had to go on to the Philippines with a load of mines. We took those out, and they said, "Also, we want you to put an amphibian plane on board, and on your return trip, we want you to conduct a survey of Wake Island lagoon, principally the western end of it, to find out whether our flying boats of this vintage can land in there safely."

The captain called me up and gave me the job of going down to the hydrographic office in Honolulu and getting all the information I could on Wake Island. The most recent information that I could discover there was the charts made by the British in 1839, the last instance of anybody ever having been on Wake Island, on which had been established a rescue emergency supply of food. Some Japanese ship had wrecked and gone in there somewhere around 1910, and that was the last time anybody had any record of anybody being on Wake Island.

We worked out the plan for coordination with the mapping service in the air, and I had the job of soundings in the boats that we acquired on our cruise, some in Honolulu, some in the Philippines. These were little pulling boats--16 feet was the biggest one we had. We took stadimeter angles from markers to the big marker that we had on the map, for planes to see on their mapping processes. That gave us air and surface correlation between the marks, so that the soundings that we put down could be located properly with the surrounding islands.

We completed our survey and put the map together and put the soundings on them, and it was all finished before we got back to Pearl Harbor.

Q: Did you get any augmentation of personnel to help with the survey?

Admiral Keith: Well, only the air people. We put an amphibian plane on board, the people that manned that, and the people who ran the cameras--they were all new. But the rest of it was a very simple process to locate where a boat was, relative to the island. That was no difficulty.

One interesting thing. Captain Markland, who was later on captain of the West Virginia, was an ordnance postgraduate student, quite an intelligent thinker.[*] He asked me to find out if anybody in the crew had an old-fashioned alarm clock. So I went around, and I found some old chief that had an alarm clock. The captain specified, "I want the kind that when you wind it up, the key starts turning around and runs down and down, until the spring says, 'We ain't going to run you any longer.'"

He took that, and he made a pantograph, put it in a box, and ran a graph paper around it with a pin on his pantograph. He used that to run almost 48 hours' worth of tide gauge readings. This thing moved up and down with a float on the tide. It was the only mid-Pacific tide reading that was extant in those days. So he had added a little bit of knowledge to the world. If you'll go and look at Mr. Bowditch, he'd tell you there's only one tide a day in the middle of the Pacific Ocean. At Wake Island, Captain Martin verified what Mr. Nathaniel Bowditch had to say.[†]

Q: What was your job in that ship?

Admiral Keith: Communication officer. I was sent two coded messages. Both were about Wake Island. I got a discrepancy on both of them. While I was over ashore, my Keith-trained coding board made a mistake, and we got a discrepancy. I was certainly not a communicator, and didn't want to be. I mentioned that the captain was an ordnance PG. He said to me--whether this is oral history or not--when I explained it to him, "Keith, the more I hear about communications, the prouder I am of my ignorance of it."

---

[*] Captain Henry T. Markland, USN, commanded the USS West Virginia (BB-48) from 5 January 1940 to 12 August 1941. He held the rank of commander as skipper of the Nitro.
[†] Nathaniel Bowditch (1773-1838) was an American mathematician and astronomer.

I said, "Captain, sometimes you must almost bust the buttons off your shirt." [Laughter] We had a good time together.

Q: How much of your time in that ship was spent replenishing ammunition in combatant ships?

Admiral Keith: None at sea.

Q: I didn't think at sea, but you probably did it in port sometimes, didn't you?

Admiral Keith: No. No. This was purely a process of transferring one kind of ammunition from a depot, where it was probably manufactured, to another ammunition depot, or distributing the product of a manufacturing area to the various areas of need around in the various supply ammunition depots.

Q: Then where did the battleships, cruisers, and destroyers get their ammunition?

Admiral Keith: Well, it was brought out to you on barges from Norfolk, from the ammunition depot up the Elizabeth River, for instance. To tell you where they all were now in various ports is an impossibility for me.

Q: But essentially, they had to go to the ammunition depot to get it.

Admiral Keith: This was part of the supply depot's job. When it was time for you to replenish ammunition, you got in touch with the people that had the ammunition. They arranged for the ammunition depot to put it on barges, and a tug brought them out and came alongside. It was an all-hands evolution to take your cranes and put the shells down, put the big 12-inch projectiles and cans of powder down into the various places, and store them away.

But I never, in all my career, I think, was really involved, where I had to arrange to get ammunition. When I was gunnery officer on the Aylwin later, I don't think I made arrangements to get my ammunition. It might have been done by the division commander to replenish it. It wasn't my responsibility. My responsibility was to make plans for receiving the delivery barge and storing it away. That isn't a detail that really established any significance, other than it was distributed, it was available. If you had a reason to need ammunition, there was a definite chain you went through in order to get it.

Q: Was there any apprehension about allowing the Nitro into certain ports because of having ammunition on board?

Admiral Keith: No. There were, of course, safety precautions. You had stevedoring gangs whose contracts required that they unload you. Our ship's force was much more adept at handling the ammunition winches on those ships; they were all steam-driven. They could sling that stuff around like nobody's business. The sailorman was expert. These stevedore crews that came on board didn't have the same desire to get the job done that the sailor did. When the sailor got through, he went on liberty. But if the stevedoring crew took two days instead of one, that was just that much more pay for them. Anytime that the Nitro could get into port with a sailing date where the stevedores were not available and use our own ship's company to handle whatever the ammunition situation required, we would do it. We'd get in on Saturdays and get out Saturday night anytime we could, so not to have to bother with the stevedoring unions.

Q: It's interesting that the incentives for those two groups were so opposite.

*   *   *

Then I went to PG School. I wanted to be an ordnance PG. They took one look at my math marks and said, "You will go into the applied communications group." Well, in all PG courses in those days, they put more people in for the first year, where everybody took much the same general course of refresher in navigation, in engineering, in electricity, and things of this kind. Then you went on to a further year, or maybe two, to get your degree and graduate as an engineer in ordnance or communications or whatever it might be. Some people then went on to Michigan State, to Columbia University, and various other places, to further their studies, particularly in ordnance and gunnery.

Q: Was that considered the general line course the first year?

Admiral Keith: That became the general line course. At mid-year, if my memory serves me, we had 24 people going into the applied communications course, and 16 of them were to be the ones who went on to finish the applied communications. The other eight were shifted over; eight from ordnance and eight from engineering shifted over to go into the general line course. Your first shore duty was usually two years, and the second year of shore duty would be somewhere else besides the PG school.

I was selected to go on in applied communications. I think I made some comment a little while ago that I wasn't very much of a communicator. I went down to see the executive officer of the PG School. I told him that I had spent my seven years at sea in gunnery, four years in turrets, and then the two year-tour with the <u>Overton</u> was all gunnery, torpedoes, first lieutenant job. All of those were my jobs in one hat for two years on there. Then I had been exposed to communications on the <u>Nitro</u>. After all that, I felt that I had a career that was sadly lacking in engineering experience, and that if I were going anywhere in the Navy, I had to get some engineering experience. So I begged to be excused.

He talked to my boss in the communication world, and he talked to me and tried to dissuade me. I stood by my guns, and they respected my request. They let me go into the general line course and finish that during the second half of the year in Annapolis.

*   *   *

It wasn't until I was there in the PG School in '35 that I began to think about damage control. What made me think about it was that I was required to write a thesis or make a speech on some naval character, and I selected von Tirpitz, who built the Kaiser's navy.* Long before the Titanic proved that watertight doors built below the waterline sometimes didn't get closed, he had eliminated any passage below the waterline in the German battleships and cruisers--no inter-connection.† If you wanted to inspect this side of a bulkhead, you had to climb up here and go down on that side.

When I was inspecting in the Arizona and in the Utah, I was aware of an officer that had asphyxiated while inspecting a tank in the Texas, so we ventilated properly. I griped like hell that they made me climb way up here and go down here, until I read about von Tirpitz and his sagacity. I wasn't aware of the reason for my having to go so far to get such a short distance.

Going to lectures and trying to learn more about the service, I went to one or two Marine briefings before World War II had even started, in which their estimates of casualties for a landing would be 50% over the beach. In your first wave you'd lose 50% of your men to wounds. I don't think in World War II we ever had--even in Tarawa we didn't have that many casualties, so we had learned lessons there.

* * *

After PG School, I had a year at the Naval Observatory in the time service.‡ This was a very interesting experience, because an astronomer named Clements and an astronomer named Salzburg at the Naval Observatory had developed a system of measuring stars, transiting at the zenith in Washington, D.C. The zenith always seemed to be just a little bit clearer than stars transiting just on your meridian, going through Washington. Your chance of getting an observation on them was, therefore, a little surer than the way they used to do it.

What they did was to develop a little motor that drove a plate at the same rate of transit that the star was apparently moving over into the zenith and through it, so that you

---

* Admiral Alfred von Tirpitz was State Secretary of Navy from 1898 to 1916, during which time he created the fleet used by Kaiser Wilhelm II in fighting World War I. The World War II battleship Tirpitz was named for him.
† In April 1912, during her maiden voyage, the British passenger liner Titanic struck an iceberg in the North Atlantic and sank as a result of progressive flooding.
‡ The Naval Observatory is off Massachusetts Avenue in northwest Washington, D.C.

started to get a picture here, and you reversed your motor. Then you turned the plate around and got one picture here, one picture here, and one picture here, and one picture here, which, using right ascension and declination, you could determine precisely how far those dots were off of the true zenith. They applied that to time and worked it out.

They took a photograph by reflecting the light from the star, transiting it to zenith, into a mercury basin 18 feet down a tube, back up to the moving plate on their motor-driven photographic equipment. It was a very interesting thing, and they had done a wonderful job. They could measure time, then, to one-thousandth of a second, and it was remarkable how many people were interested in time to the most precise that you could possibly get.

In the Navy, the precision time users were the surveyors. In those days, we had survey ships in various parts of the world, trying to establish the position, or to confirm the position, of islands as well on the chart as the latitude and longitude marks. With the establishment of time to this precision, they changed the position of some of the islands in the Caribbean and around Panama, the fortified islands out there and up the coast of Panama, on up to Nicaragua, by as much as two miles. The details of that, I couldn't give you, but the fact is that these were established, and it is available in the history of the Naval Observatory in Washington. So this was very, very interesting.

I worked with astronomers all that summer, taking the place of one of them on this tube or this observation station, while the astronomers got leave. This was the reason that the young ensigns were being rotated through this job for a year, after they came out of the general line course, so that the astronomers could get some leave once in a while, because their work had to go on.

The result of that was I got a promotion examination while I was in Washington from lieutenant (junior grade) to lieutenant. I took 11 promotion examinations. One of them had to do with solving astronomical navigation problems. What they did with the people who were appearing before the statutory board in Washington was to put in new questions and use the officers there as guinea pigs. They wanted to see whether the questions were too tough for them to send out into the fleet, where examinations were given also. If you failed them out in the fleet, you got six months' time to study and take them over again without losing seniority. But when you were on shore duty, you were supposed to have plenty of time to study, and if you missed once, you lost six months right then in seniority.

This particular question was given to two lieutenants going up for lieutenant commander--one Hal Baker and one Pete Weeden--and to Taylor Keith.[*] It required that you cross the equator and the 180th meridian at the same time and take a moon sight. We all three got 4.0's on it: they because they were smart, and I because I was working at the Naval Observatory and was up to snuff on navigation. But I'm sure somewhere in the fleet, when that problem went out, there were people that were unhappy with it. Because you had to extrapolate from the northern hemisphere to the southern hemisphere to get any readings of the moon, and they didn't have enough information down there to give you southern hemisphere information in the nautical almanac. Well, these were times long ago.

Q: At what point in this sequence had you gotten married?

Admiral Keith: While I was at the Postgraduate School.

Q: Where had you met your future wife?

Admiral Keith: I had met her when I was in Norfolk during that ten-month overhaul period in the Overton. Every time you ask me a question, it reminds me of something, and it's funny to me. It's not history, but it's good, interesting stuff for somebody that wants to hear how somebody grows up.

My wife was an Episcopalian. She wanted to get married in church; she wanted to have bridesmaids. The only time that I had any leave after we decided to get married was for Easter vacation, which is right in the middle of Lent. In the Episcopal Church, they wouldn't allow her to have a big wedding. We could have been married in the church. Well, we decided to get married on our Washington's birthday holiday.[†] So we did. It was

---
[*] Lieutenant Harold D. Baker, USN; Lieutenant William W. Weeden, Jr., USN.
[†] On 22 February 1936, Keith married Eleanor Langhorne Hudgins in Norfolk, Virginia.

a Saturday, and I got off on Friday and went down to Norfolk, got married. We came home.

At 8:15 Monday morning, I was in a review course in electricity with Tony Lacazza, one of the famous professors of the PG School, as my instructor. At 8:16 that morning, he said, "Mr. Keith, would you discourse on [some electrical problem]?"

Everybody in the class just whooped and hollered! So I went up to Tony after class to tell him that I'd been married Saturday night, and he understood then why everybody laughed.

Q: You hadn't done too much studying.

Admiral Keith: No. Long years after that, I went to speak to the graduating class at the Postgraduate School in Monterey.* This was in the early 1960s, when I was commander of the First Fleet. They had a luncheon after graduation exercises, and there were many people there. Among them was Admiral Overesch, retired, who had been commandant of midshipmen when I was on duty at the Naval Academy the first time, and Admiral Spruance, and also Tony Lacazza, who was being honored that day because that was his last day as a member of the faculty of the Postgraduate School, after 25 or 30 years there.† At the luncheon, they asked me if I would talk about my experience of talking to the Communists in Korea. The superintendent said, "Admiral Keith said really he didn't think that people wanted to hear him talk, but he's agreed to talk."

So my opening remarks were that I wasn't really reluctant to talk, but I was reluctant to talk in such august company. Being a fresh-caught young admiral, I could see so many faces around the room that had much greater experience than I would be able to talk about, but that there were two people in that audience that I wanted particularly to comment on. One of them was a Navy boss of mine who would be astounded that Keith

---

* Originally established at Annapolis on 9 June 1909, the Naval Postgraduate School was moved to the grounds of the former Hotel Del Monte in Monterey, California, in June 1951.
† Vice Admiral Harvey E. Overesch, USN (Ret.) Admiral Raymond A. Spruance, USN (Ret.) was Commander Fifth Fleet during World War II and president of the Naval War College in the late 1940s.

ever was reluctant to talk, because when he knew me, I was always having something to say to him. Then I told the story about Tony Lacazza, that here I was a dumb-mute, as far as Tony was concerned, when he called on me to talk. Well, that got me off to a good start in my talk, anyhow. That's not history, but it's still something that I remember, and it's associated with people that I knew about.

* * *

When I left my first shore duty and went to sea, I had a tour as flag lieutenant for Admiral Carleton Watts.[*] He was commander of the old Base Force, which was the supply train and so forth of our Navy of the '30s and '40s. This was an experience that added a lot to my knowledge of the Navy and the way things got done.

The first person to pay a call was the executive officer from the PG School. He was the first official caller on his boss, Admiral Watts, when I got there. Here I was, after I had said to this exec that I was hell-bent to get some engineering duty. Instead, I was standing up there flag lieutenanting. He looked at me, and this grin came all over his face. "I see you're heavily involved in engineering duty, Keith." [Laughter]

Under Admiral Watts, I wrote a letter for him once, and I used the Latin phrase vice versa. However, instead of writing "vice versa" in my letter, I used good Brooklynese; I said "visa versa." I took the letter in for him to sign, and he looked up at me and said, "Sailor, how sure are you of your Latin?"

I said, "I'm not positive, sir."

He said, "If you're going to use it, I think you ought to be sure that what you write is good. Take a look at it."

I went back, got my dictionary, and I had put "visa versa" in my lexicon, instead of "vice versa." But you listen. How many people you hear talking, how many people you hear even on television, that use that and say "visa versa." There's no such word.

Q: Another one that's commonly mispronounced is by people who say "forté," when they mean "forte."

---

[*] Rear Admiral William Carleton Watts, USN.

Admiral Keith: I did that sitting right there on that sofa last night, and my wife said, "Forte!" like that at me. That's funny that you mention it, because for some reason, when I was reviewing certain things with her last night that I wanted to talk about, that was one of the things I did.

As the admiral's flag lieutenant, I had a lot of extra duties that I took on or was assigned, because being a flag lieutenant didn't keep you very busy. It was a stay-put job, not a lot of signaling to do or things of this kind. One of the things I did was run the shore patrol for the Long Beach area, or wherever the fleet happened to be if it moved. By this time we were given some permanent shore patrol officers that helped us establish a system of handling cases and not to just do it hit-or-miss, by having the Arizona ordered to send a lieutenant and four men ashore, and the Pennsylvania to do the same thing, and somebody else to do something else. So nobody had any experience; they were just there. Now you had experienced patrol officers that took charge and ran the show.

Q: Was this set up near the fleet landing at Pico Street?

Admiral Keith: Yes. That was the headquarters in that area. The city of Long Beach gave us a place to operate from. I also ran the athletic fields: Trona Field and the one at Long Beach that the city gave us. The responsibility for that belonged to the fleet commander, and he had people on his staff who had that responsibility. It was delegated to the Base Force, which was most always in port to do the job. Through that connection, I had an opportunity to come to know Forrest Sherman, who subsequently was CNO. He was then on the staff as a commander.[*] I came to know General So-and-so of the Marine Corps, who was afterwards a distinguished commander of the Marines in battle.

Q: What are your impressions of Forrest Sherman from that period?

---

[*] Commander Forrest P. Sherman, USN, was the aviator on the staff of Commander in Chief U.S. Fleet. As an admiral, Sherman served as Chief of Naval Operations from 1949 to 1951.

Admiral Keith: Oh, I felt about him, I guess, the way everybody else did. He was a man who could make a decision. But my job was so relatively minor that when I went to see him, I could say, "We can do this or we can do that, and if we do this, this is what I think we should do."

He'd say, "Do it." So there was no hassle about it. There was not a major decision, something about running the athletic program, doing this or doing that. At the same time, I did have a chance to see him and talk to him.

When we went to Panama on the fleet problem in 1939, Mame Kelly ran afoul of my patrol officer, and she let the B-girls come from the dance floor out to the bar and ask the sailors to buy them a drink. If a sailor bought them a drink, they'd charge him what they'd charge inside the dance hall for dancing with a sailor and sitting at his table with him for a drink. So instead of the drink being, let's say, 50 cents out here, we found that they were putting the prices at $2.00 or $1.75, or something, which was an outlandish increase.

My patrol officer got hold of me on board the flagship and said, "Unless you direct otherwise, I'm going to go there and tell them unless they put their prices on the bar as to what drinks cost and charge them at the bar, I'm going to put a patrol outside and ain't any sailors going in there."[*]

I said, "Go ahead."

The next morning, I went over to the Pennsylvania and went to see Sherman.[†] I said, "Last night I got a telephone call from a patrol officer, and he told me what had happened and that you were going to do this unless I thought otherwise. I said, 'Go ahead.' I hope you approve."

"Right on." No questions. He accepted what we'd done as being the proper thing, and that he would have okayed it if he'd been there.

Q: Was he a friendly individual?

---

[*] The Base Force flagship was the USS Argonne (AS-10).
[†] The USS Pennsylvania (BB-38) was the flagship of Commander in Chief U.S. Fleet, Admiral Claude C. Bloch, USN.

Admiral Keith: Oh, sure. I see his wife now. She comes out here once in a while to visit a friend. She was a horsewoman. I came from the town of Warrenton, Virginia, which was right in what is known as horse country. She was showing in the oldest horse show in America, which is in Upperville, Virginia. Always, when I was at home, I used to go to the horse show. I saw many friends and saw beautiful horses. I used to ride when I was a youth.

I walked in one day, and there was Forrest Sherman, leaning over the rail, watching the show ring. We stopped and had a talk. Perfectly normal. I mean, he was by then CNO, I guess, and I was a captain. But there he was in civilian clothes, I was in civilian clothes. We talked as old friends, and he asked me what my interest in horses was. I said, "I grew up on them, sir." It turned out that his wife was stabling her horse with a first cousin of mine, so we talked about my cousin. We didn't know any of this then, so my relationship with Admiral Sherman was one of admiration for what he accomplished, for his ability to analyze a situation, which he did during the war, for Nimitz, and to make a decision that was well-reasoned.[*]

Q: Apparently he had quite a remarkable intellect.

Admiral Keith: He did. I wasn't testing his intellect, but you can tell when they've got it. There's no question about the people. Well, Bloch had a remarkable staff.[†] He had Fairfax Leary as his chief of staff, who, I would say, if anything, was the weakest one.[‡] Another was Admiral Noble, who went on to be Chief of the BuOrd, commanded a cruiser in the war.[§]

---

[*] Fleet Admiral Chester W. Nimitz, USN, Commander in Chief Pacific Fleet and Pacific Ocean Areas, 1941-45.
[†] Admiral Bloch served as Commander in Chief U.S. Fleet from January 1938 to January 1940.
[‡] Captain Herbert Fairfax Leary, USN.
[§] Commander Albert G. Noble, USN, was the fleet gunnery officer. As a rear admiral, Noble was Chief of the Bureau of Ordnance from 1947 to 1950.

Q: When you had this shore patrol duty in Long Beach, how well-behaved would you say the sailors of that era were?

Admiral Keith: Not much different from sailors anywhere, any time. Some of them are going to misbehave, some of them aren't.

Q: Was drunk and disorderly the main complaint?

Admiral Keith: Sometimes.

Well, let me talk about the actions of my friend Charlie Moore. He was my permanent shore patrol officer in Panama, and again in Norfolk, when they took the fleet in there in the spring of 1939. He found out that people at a bar down on main street were charging civilians 25 cents for near-beer, which was legal in Virginia, and they was charging sailors 75 and 90 cents for the same drink. Charlie put a shore patrol outside that door and said, "When you get the signs so that they let every patrol know what the prices are, I'll let some sailors back in your place." So I learned my lesson as to how to deal with these situations.

Q: You talked about the athletic competition at Trona Field. How valuable was that in the prewar years for morale purposes?

Admiral Keith: Certain ships always seemed to win. The Tennessee had a great athletic program. The Maryland always did well in athletics. California usually did well. I'm sure that was a morale builder, that the sailors would always bet. But for the ones that never could get off a dime with their athletics, I don't think it was much of a thing. The Utah won the race boat in the Atlantic once. I had a good baseball team on the Utah. We weren't in the class with the Wright. They had the pick of all the aviator baseball players and assigned them to the Wright, which was a tender. Those were the days when the Saratoga and the Lexington were the only carriers we had, and they were out here.

Q: There was some tremendous betting on the Battenberg Cup races.

Admiral Keith: Well, that was for the boat races.* It was a means of keeping the sailors away from the bars. The Navy always astounded me. When they took the fleet to Panama, they would grant liberty at 1:00 o'clock in the afternoon, and it ended at 5:00 in the afternoon. They had to start back to the ship at 5:00 o'clock. Well, it got them off the streets, but it also limited how far they could go. When liberty began, they filled the bars from those nearest to the fleet landing to the ones farthest from it, in progression as to how they landed. The first got the first, and the last got the last. By 5:00 o'clock, they all had their fill, and you had a procession of drunks being shepherded back by shore patrol to the landing.

Then you got experience as boat officer. You'd take 50-foot motor launches and 40-foot motor launches in and fill them up. If you were lucky, you'd get everybody from the same ship to take back to their ship out in the roads, out off the fortified islands of Panama. If you were unlucky, you would get people from the Arkansas and the Florida or the Utah and the Florida, who disliked each other, and then they would start a fight, and you'd have a wing-ding on your hands. You were the guy responsible for it.

We never, until we had the shore patrol in 1939, ever allowed sailors in Guantanamo to go into Cuba. Again, I talked to Forrest Sherman and said, "The Cubans would like us to have liberty up there. What do you think about it?"

He said, "I think it's worth a try."

So we started granting liberty up there. We formed a team of doctors and inspected the ladies every week. We made it pretty clear that we weren't going to stand for a lot of hooliganism, that we had patrols that were up there. The sailors appreciated the fact that you gave them some privileges with an expectation that they were going to live up to it, and they did. Another lesson that you learned: you treat them like children and peons and expect them to obey every order, they're going to beat you any way they can. You give

---

* The cup went to the ship whose oarsmen pulled their boat fastest in races against the crews from other ships.

them their head and expect that they're going to behave themselves, they will--with few exceptions.

The Base Force had two other experiences that I remember because of the great changes that had come. We were in charge of a landing to be made by Marines at Maui, if my memory serves me right. We had 50-foot motor launches and 40-foot motor launches, the only vehicles to get anybody ashore. We had some high winds and rough seas, and we lost a good many boats, and we injured some people. We didn't lose any lives. Sabin was the operations officer for the Base Force, and he was in charge of this.* I was his assistant, finding extra work to do. But we proceeded from this in 1937 to the LSTs and the LCIs, which we developed, I think, because that landing made such a deep impression on people that they started thinking about how they were going to get troops ashore without upsetting those cumbersome, unmanageable, great big motor launches.†

Another thing the Base Force of that vintage was required to do was to conduct fueling operations at sea. I came into this at the other end of it, because we had started the planning of it when I was on the Base Force staff with Sabe, and when they actually did it in the next fleet exercise, I was in the Aylwin.‡ But we had the oilers proceeding at six knots into the wind, and approaches were made at the most sedate pace you've ever seen. It would take about 15 to 20 minutes for each ship to get up to go alongside, and they were way out here somewhere, and every stadimeter on the ship was going and calling out ranges. Everything on the tanker that could provide an angle was giving angles for the bridge peloruses to read off to the conning officer. It was really quite a fracas. A couple of years later, we were fueling downwind alongside at 15 knots.

Q: Didn't they initially start off with throwing over a towline, too, during the underway replenishment?

---

* Lieutenant Commander Lorenzo S. Sabin, Jr., USN.
† LSTs--tank landing ships; LCIs--landing craft infantry. These were landing craft used for amphibious landings during World War II.
‡ USS Aylwin (DD-355) was commissioned 1 March 1935. She had a standard displacement of 1,375 tons, was 341 feet long, and 34 feet in the beam. Her design speed was 37 knots. She was armed with five 5-inch guns and eight 21-inch torpedo tubes.

Admiral Keith: I'm sure they did. They tried everything.

Q: That was really some of the early experimental work on it.

Admiral Keith: That's right. But that was done where two large ships were doing it, not destroyers.

Q: I see.

Admiral Keith: I think the slow approach that I'm talking about was the destroyers' method. They had a towline and trailed a fuel hose over the stern, which still was used a lot by the British Navy in World War II. We had a hard time getting them to switch over to alongside fueling.

Q: You have to walk before you can run, and this was the walking stage in the late '30s.

Admiral Keith: Well, that was just how far we were in lack of foresight or what, but if you're going to put a fleet at sea, these were the things that you had to do.*

Q: What do you recall about the Argonne as a flagship?

Admiral Keith: Not a great deal. I was in charge of the band, and I had an ex-German flame-thrower from World War I as the bandmaster. He gave a concert every day on the deck outside of the wardroom during the noon hour. I had him learn the complete tunes for all the little ditties that were played on the radio to introduce various programs, and I had a

---

* For details on the progress, see Thomas Wildenberg, Gray Steel and Black Oil: Fast Tankers and Replenishment at Sea in the U.S. Navy, 1912-1992 (Annapolis: Naval Institute Press, 1996).

list of them published so that people would learn what the name of the opera, the music that this particular little ditty came from. It was a very interesting program.

Argonne stayed in port, and when she went to sea, it was a great occasion.

Q: She would have been a comfortable ship to live aboard. I think she was a liner before that, wasn't she?

Admiral Keith: Something like that.[*] She had a staircase, I'm sure. They finally put my desk right in that stairwell, and I sat next to Captain Tisdale, who took over when they upgraded Sabin's job from lieutenant commander operations officer in the Base Force to a captain's job.[†] We had a desk here in one side of a cage, and the other here on this side.

Q: Several people I've talked to have spoken very highly of him. What are your recollections?

Admiral Keith: I'm a great admirer of Chip Tisdale, and he liked me. I mean, we sat side by side each other--a great deal of difference in rank, but we came to know each other. It's my feeling that, certainly, rank has its privileges, certainly rank deserves respect for their accomplishments, but there's no need to stand in awe of somebody because he's an admiral. He's a human being, and he thinks properly, and you can talk to him.

*   *   *

In the spring of 1939, before I left the Base Force, we took drones down to Guantanamo, where we provided them for all sorts of practices out there. I think maybe some destroyers got to shoot down there; I'm not real sure. But I know that all the battleships fired their port batteries and their starboard batteries at drones.

Antiaircraft fire wasn't too accurate in 1939. So that as they would open up with a starboard battery, they would be short. The radio operator in the air, flying this drone, off

---

[*] When initially commissioned in the Navy in 1921, the Argonne was a personnel transport, hull number AP-4.
[†] Captain Mahlon S. Tisdale, USN.

on the horizon somewhere, was just as well aware that that salvo was short, and he was just as well aware that they were going to spot out. So whenever he saw a short salvo, he changed course toward the salvo, and they spotted out, and it went over, and so he knew they were coming back in that he changed course to the right. They fired and fired and fired, battleship after battleship, and none of them ever knocked a drone down.

If they did, it was happenstance, until the Maryland got its chance to fire. She'd always had a pretty good reputation in gunnery, so they took the forward battery and put an out-spot on it from what their solution was. They took the after 5-inch battery and put an in-spot on it, and then they decided how close they were in spotted on from that. Then, because the guy was straddled, he couldn't make any change in course. The second salvo knocked him out of the air. Well, we just cheered! Being surface sailors, you know, on the old Argonne, when we heard finally that the Maryland knocked them down, and when we heard how they had done it, we thought that was one of the smartest things we'd ever heard.

Q: That was very clever.

Admiral Keith: [Laughter] Anyhow . . .

Q: I think it's worth pointing out that this is strictly visual fire control. You had no radar yet at that point on your director.

Admiral Keith: You had optical rangefinders. But one of the things that the Utah did after she became a target ship and an experimental ship, was to have a battery on there for development of this new gun that was going to go into the fleet, the 5-inch/38. After exhaustive tests, they came out with a report that you could have very accurate gunfire and that you could plot the bursts as long as you had continuous range finding. Then you could analyze the bursts to see why you were over or why you were short from your range-finding.

Well, on a battleship, your range finder was far away from the guns, up in the mast somewhere, and it was a steady platform. But when you moved that range finder into the bridge of a destroyer and started shooting four or five 5-inch guns at the same time, the range finder was going like this, and from the opening of gunfire to the last gun firing, there wasn't a range on that target drone or target or anything else that was worth a damn. So all the things that we were required to do to plot those bursts after every antiaircraft fire, that was a lot of who-struck-John; it was a lot of work for the gunnery officer.

* * *

I came in on the Aylwin to overhaul in Mare Island.[*] My captain went over with the other three skippers, and the admiral was Pluvy Kempff.[†] He said he had had a great deal of trouble with the bars in Vallejo. He told us that they were just sousing his sailors with drink, and the sailors were getting into trouble. He needed a good man from our outfit to run the shore patrol over there for a couple of weeks. My captain immediately jumped up and said, "I'll send you a lieutenant, sir." He didn't know anything about my shore patrol background, but he had a lieutenant gunnery officer, and he had a lieutenant chief engineer, and you know, when you're going into overhaul, which one of those individuals in indispensable on board the ship, and that's the chief engineer.

So it became Keith's duty to do it. I was told to go and report to Admiral Kempff and to take over the shore patrol. He said, "Young man, I want you to get this Vallejo bar situation straightened out. I don't want any more reports of drunkenness, misbehaving sailors. You get going and get it straightened out, if you have to walk the streets all night."

I went in and asked to see the proprietor of every bar on the main street in Vallejo and up the two side streets. I told them that the admiral was very unhappy with the fact that they were selling liquor to sailors who obviously had had enough to drink, and that my patrol was going to be around. If they found them serving a drink to any sailor who obviously had had too much to drink, there wasn't going to be another sailor in there as

---

[*] For repairs and maintenance, the Aylwin went to the Mare Island Navy Yard, Vallejo, California.
[†] Rear Admiral Clarence F. Kempff, USN, was Commandant of the Navy yard and of the 12th Naval District.

long as I was on patrol. I said, "Not only for tonight, but as long as I'm on patrol, we're going to stop this business. If you don't get their money tonight, you'll get it tomorrow night or the next night. Don't be a pig and try to get it all at once."

So I made the rounds. One night I was walking down the street, and I heard a rumpus inside. I went in, and the owner came running over to me, and he said, "We did not serve this man too much to drink. He was sitting over there in that booth with his girl, or his lady, and somebody at the bar said something, and he picked up a glass and whammed him over the head with it. He didn't have too much to drink. We're very careful." So he pled and pled.

I said, "Okay, it looks to me as if you're right, if he was here and he hit somebody at the bar."

So another night I was on patrol, and I saw this sailor walking down the street after he'd obviously had too much to drink. So the patrol and I got him, and we put him in a taxi and told him to go back to Mare Island. He rode on down the street a few blocks, then told the taxi driver to turn to the right. We followed on down, and he came back around the corner, having gotten out of the taxi, and ran into us. He took off and ran across the street and up the stairs into a house of ill repute, which I had also visited and made the same statement to the madam. She met me at the top of the steps, and she came running. "He's in Mabel's room, under the bed!" [Laughter]

Now, do you think this is history?

Q: Sure. Social history.

Admiral Keith: Well, that's the kind of sailors we had.

*   *   *

The original Hawaiian Detachment went to Hawaii in the fall of 1939. I was gunnery officer of the Aylwin, which was part of it. The Enterprise was the base of it, and we had two cruiser divisions. Adolphus Andrews was the admiral.[*] We were all aware that he had strict orders out, that he would go ashore and confer one Thursday morning with the Army commanding general, and the next Thursday morning on board the Indianapolis, which was his flagship.

Q: That was the Scouting Force flagship, yes.

Admiral Keith: Well, he was commander of the original Hawaiian Detachment, which was not Scouting Force.[†] That was the Hawaiian Detachment. That was ordered on a Saturday afternoon from Washington to Admiral Bloch--prepare and sail a carrier, two squadrons of destroyers, and two divisions of cruisers.[‡] But we got out. On Saturday afternoon, we were provisioned and on our way on Wednesday, if my memory serves me right.[§] We didn't know why we were ordered out there. We never did know. But it was very, very specific that every week there would be a conference between the Navy commander and the Army commander, with their staffs. They discussed their situation and what they were responsible for and what they were going to do.

Then the fleet came out on a fleet problem, and the fleet stayed.[**] That moved

---

[*] Vice Admiral Adolphus Andrews, USN, served as Commander Scouting Force from 1938 to 1941.

[†] Admiral Andrews held both duties simultaneously until the spring of 1940, when many of the fleet's major combatants moved to Hawaii and the so-called Hawaiian Detachment was absorbed back into the fleet.

[‡] For the text of the message establishing the Hawaiian Detachment, see James O. Richardson and George C. Dyer, On the Treadmill to Pearl Harbor (Washington, D.C.: Naval History Division, 1973), page 162.

[§] The Aylwin left the Mare Island Navy Yard on Wednesday, 11 October 1939, and arrived at Pearl Harbor on 18 October as the Hawaiian Detachment came into being.

[**] Fleet Problem XXI took place in the Hawaiian area in the spring of 1940. When it was completed, President Franklin D. Roosevelt directed that the fleet remain at Pearl Harbor rather than return to its bases on the West Coast. The idea was that leaving the fleet in Hawaii would serve as a deterrent to Japanese aggression in the Far East.

Admiral Richardson into the position as senior officer afloat, instead of Vice Admiral Andrews.*

Q: That was in the spring of 1940.

Admiral Keith: That's correct. The young officers and some of the skippers in the destroyer force played softball. We'd play against Wheeler Field, and we'd play against Hickam, and we came to know a great many of the young people in the Army Air Corps out there through these games. Several times on Saturday, I'd be in the PX, and I'd meet one of the young Army Air Corps wives, and say, "Where's Bill? Where's Joe?"

They would go into a snit and a tirade, and say, "For the umpteenth week in a row, all the planes have been deployed to outlying fields. They're not at home. They never are on the weekend anymore." Well, this then became known to us, that all the fighter planes were out at Bellows Field or in Maui, or somewhere else other than at their bases at Hickam and Wheeler.

So when the Japanese strike came, it gradually became known that most of the planes were in the center of the field, with them riding herd around them like a bunch of cowboys herding their cattle. It seemed that the only thing that the military forces in Hawaii were concerned about was sabotage.

Well, by December 7, I'd gone to shore. But I'll jump from those days to my days in 1950, when I was in Hawaii as training group commander there. Sam Morison came out to deliver a series of 14 lectures to the Navy personnel or Army personnel there.† He gave them sometimes in a Navy theater, sometimes in an Army theater. He also gave the same lectures a few nights later at the University of Hawaii.

On one or two occasions, I didn't hear the lecture given to the military, and I went to the University of Hawaii. The difference in the attitude of the audience is something I

---

* Admiral James O. Richardson, USN, served as Commander in Chief U.S. Fleet from 6 January 1940 to 1 February 1941.
† Captain Samuel Eliot Morison, USNR, was then in the process of writing his 14-volume series History of United States Naval Operations in World War II.

just want to make a comment about. Morison was talking to commanders, sitting down in his audience at the military bases, about whom he was speaking--people like Soc McMorris and Frog Low.* There was a buzz of conversation when he would say favorable or unfavorable things about the people in his audience, but he spoke his mind, and he was talking right from his 14 volumes of naval history in World War II.

Then I'd go to the University of Hawaii to pick up a lecture that I'd missed, and you could hear a pin drop. Here was this group of Eurasian people collected there because they wanted to learn as much as they could, and they didn't move a muscle. They sat and were completely attentive to what Morison was having to say.

Well, with 14 lectures and standing around afterwards, you came to know people pretty well, and I had an opportunity to ask Admiral Morison my question. My question was predicated on what I have told you now as to the deployment of the airplanes, the riding herd on them. I said that there was ammunition when I was there, that every sector of the gun areas for Pearl Harbor was prescribed, and if a division of destroyers had this sector sail, they moved a destroyer in to take up that buoy, so that that sector at least had one gun in there to shoot in that area. All of this changed between June '41, when I went ashore, and December 7, 1941.

So this is, to me today, still a puzzle. It was a puzzle to me and to us then. I asked Sam Morison, "Please, sir, can you throw any light on this?"

He said, "Captain, I think I had free access to the Navy records, and I can find nothing that throws any light on the change from ammunition at the readiness, which was when you were talking about, and the protection against sabotage situation, which existed on December the seventh. I can find nothing that gave anyone any instructions along that line. No messages, no orders, nothing. I don't hear anything in the testimony of the committees that investigated it that throws any light on it." As far as I know, there's still no light on it today.

---

* Rear Admiral Charles H. McMorris, USN, was then Commandant of the 14th Naval District; he had been Pacific Fleet plans officer during World War II. Rear Admiral Francis S. Low, USN, was then Commander Western Sea Frontier; in World War II he had been Tenth Fleet chief of staff.

On the Aylwin I had an excellent fire controlman named Suturowski, and he stayed after I left.* I have read somewhere--I don't know where I read it--that the first ship to get a shot off in Pearl Harbor, the morning of the attack, was the Aylwin.

When I was gunnery officer, I was living on board, because my wife wasn't there. Suturowski's family was back in San Diego. The two of us checked out the lineup of our gun battery every single Sunday morning when we were in port. We did it at about 7:30 or so, because we were awake, had this job to do, keep the battery lined up, and we did it. I just always guessed that Suturowski was doing the same thing, and, as I thought, all ships had ammunition up on deck at that time. Subsequently, I believe that there was a change from the dispositions that were made when I was in the fleet, to what they were at the time of December 7.

* * *

We used to have battle problems in various ships I'd served in. They'd say, "A hit in the starboard engine room," "A hit in the electrical switchboard," and so on. But they never told you what it was. So when I went to Hawaii with the original Hawaiian Detachment, they gave me the job of writing up a battle problem. So I got the blueprints out, and I said, "A hit at frame so-and-so. At frame so-and-so, this line goes through and is controlled by this switch, and this line goes through and is controlled by this switch." Or it's controlled by this circuit breaker, and all this is controlled by these circuit breakers, wherever it is. Anyhow, I assigned damage where the hit was called, and I wrote instructions to a member of the crew of the ship that was being examined, to pull these switches or to throw these switches or pull this circuit breaker, to simulate that damage.

I tested it with people, and they said, "You can throw all these switches. You're not going to do any damage." So if there was any possibility of taking a safety feature away from the ship that was maneuvering or anything of this kind, we eliminated that part of the damage. But we had actual damage, and we told the captain when we went on board to conduct these battle problems, that a member of his crew was going to be told to simulate damage by throwing certain switches, or we told the division commander. I was writing

---

* Chief Fire Controlman Edward Suturowski, USN.

this for the division commander. I told them to instruct their captains that this was the kind of battle problem they were going to get, and that their crew was to be told not to throw any switch that would hazard the ship. That we had done our best to eliminate it, but the responsibility was still the captain's.

So we gave this first battle problem, and it was on the flagship of the other division in the squadron.* We assessed a fire by putting a smoke bomb down in one of the forward trunks above the waterline that was reached by a door going through from the wardroom to the anchor chain room and then through this thing, wherever it was. But, anyhow, it was accessible, and the ship was all shut up for battle. The damage control party station, just aft of the wardroom, got the word that there was a fire in such-and-so, and so they went through the wardroom. Then they went and opened this door, and the wardroom and all the officers' rooms were filled with black, sooty smoke. The division commander and the captain's cabins, right up above the wardroom in the Aylwin class all filled up with smoke. From then on, people began to check the routes that they used to reach the damage. But it put some reality in the things, and, as far as I know, that had never been done before.

* * *

Captain Small was the observing division commander when we fired this division practice on some drones.†

Q: We didn't have the machine running when you told that, so maybe you could tell that story again, please.

Admiral Keith: When they first brought drones into the fleet, I was in the Base Force, and

---

* This was the USS Dewey DD-349), flagship of Destroyer Division One. Destroyer Division Two, the other division in DesRon One, was made up of the Aylwin (DD-355), Dale (DD-353), Farragut (DD-348), and Monaghan (DD-354).
† Captain Ernest G. Small, USN, Commander Destroyer Division Three, had the USS Drayton (DD-366) as his flagship.

the Base Force handled this. They had the utility squadrons in the fleet. They weren't under AirPac.*

The destroyers always had to fire, a duo of destroyers, at any single drone that was assigned. They couldn't waste a drone on little ships like that. But we went out for this particular practice, where we were to fire two ships and two ships. It turned out that the Monaghan ran aground off Pearl Harbor on patrol duty out there, the night before we were to sortie. There she was when we went out in the morning. First the Farragut and I, in the Aylwin, fired a practice. Even after we got in and plotted the bursts, we couldn't decide whose burst had knocked the plane down, and both Farragut and Aylwin claimed it. Then they fired the Dale, and I guess the Farragut, and they didn't hit the drone, so the drone still had some time in the air.

My division commander asked me if I'd like to shoot at it by myself. "I'm your man." As soon as I finished plotting this practice, I was going as exec of the Cushing, and my assistant gunnery officer was going to take it over. I went down and saw the captain, and said, "I'd like to let him shoot it, and I'll run the director," which he had been doing up on top of the bridge. So when we plotted the shots, the first bullet out of the first gun fired on the Aylwin hit the drone at 16,000 feet, and that's the way my new gunnery officer started out his career in gunnery.

* * *

Q: There was an interesting thing you mentioned before we started the tape that might be apropos now. You said that George Dyer, in his book with Admiral Richardson, talked about expressing surprise at being relieved. You said you were surprised to learn that Admiral Richardson claimed that.

Admiral Keith: When I was on duty in Annapolis, I knew Admiral Dyer, and I knew him well, but I don't think I've ever had a chance to ask him this question.† Because it was

---

* Air Force Pacific Fleet (AirPac) was the type command established in World War II. Previously it was known as Aircraft Battle Force.
† George C. Dyer retired as a vice admiral in 1955, at which time Keith was commandant of midshipmen at the Naval Academy. Dyer's oral history is in the Naval Institute collection.

known in the fleet, even down to the destroyer level, that Admiral Richardson had gone back to Washington, although I don't think it was ever published in any newspaper. But big ears usually find out what's going on somehow or other. I had been flag lieutenant at the same time as Tom Eddy, who was Richardson's flag lieutenant.[*]

One night, after Admiral Richardson's second visit to Washington, we were talking, and Eddy, as I remember it, said that the admiral had made two trips to Washington, trying to separate his major forces and his light forces. Eddy said that the admiral's contention was that if the basic fleet was to be based as far forward as Hawaii, that he should project light forces further into the Pacific, and base them somewhere else--Guam or Midway, or wherever. He wanted to find a place to let them anchor and get a blow once in a while, but that his statements and his explanations had not found receptive ears.[†]

Tom's dead, and I can't confirm this, but I remember him saying that Admiral Richardson had stated that he did not believe that he could continue to perform his duties as commander in chief of the fleet under the circumstances. Ergo, I felt that there should be no surprise, that when you tell the commander in chief, "I can't command under your orders as they're issued to me," that there should be no surprise in an intelligent gentleman's mind when the commander in chief finds it convenient to put somebody else in the job.[‡]

I've talked to Admiral Sabin, who was very close to Admiral Richardson. He came into the Bremerton area when Sabin was there on duty, and that he told him much the same story as I have.[§] Because, you see, I've talked about this with people who I thought had some knowledge. I knew Sabin's background with Admiral Richardson, and I asked him if he could confirm what Tom Eddy had told me. He said, "I certainly can. He said so in my

---

[*] Lieutenant Daniel T. Eddy, USN.
[†] "Getting a blow" meant taking a break from an active operating schedule.
[‡] The commander in chief referred to here is President Roosevelt, who directed that Admiral Richardson's tour of duty be cut short. He was relieved on 1 February 1941 by Admiral Husband E. Kimmel, USN.
[§] In the last months of peace and first months of war, Lieutenant Commander Sabin was serving on the staff of Commander Battleships Battle Force.

living room." He told them he couldn't continue, and yet that book right up there, if you read it, it says the admiral was surprised. Dyer was the flag secretary, I think, wasn't he?

Q: That's right. Yes, he was.

Admiral Keith: I think there must have been somebody closer to Admiral Richardson than was George Dyer. That's all I can say. I don't think he was getting the word. You don't go around and give that to George Dyer when you get back to Annapolis.

Q: No, I won't.

*   *   *

I was exec of the Cushing, and we were operating as part of the fleet out of Hawaii in 1941.[*] So many ships were in port, and so many ships were out of port. For the ones that were out of port, sometimes they would assign one ship to a ten-mile square, and you'd steam around that square, and somebody else was in another ten-mile square, and another a ten-mile square, and another destroyer. It was to conserve fuel, but at least you were under way and moving and not a sitting-duck target. But you were told that you couldn't hold swimming call. We were out there strictly for business.

I went to see the captain and said, "Sir, we've got all these life rafts on board this destroyer, and it says they hold 24 men. I just don't believe that 24 men can get in one of those life rafts. We've never tried it. I would like very much to get a group together and see what we can do to learn how to use these rafts. I want to find out how to tow them. I want to find out how many people we can get in them, what those ropes hanging down over the side are for."

So I put on my bathing trunks, and with the captain's permission I went down in the crew's quarters, where I said, "I'm looking for some volunteers to test life rafts." I had a hell of a time finding 20 men who wanted to test life rafts with me. We stopped the ship

---

[*] USS Cushing (DD-376) was commissioned 28 August 1936. She had a standard displacement of 1,500 tons, was 341 feet long, and 35 feet in the beam. Her design speed was 36 knots. She was armed with five 5-inch guns and twelve 21-inch torpedo tubes.

and put one life raft over. Some of us got out in the water, and the ship towed that life raft. We put so many men in it; we hung so many on the side. The next day we did the same thing, and I had hundreds volunteer.

Q: [Laughter] They saw how much fun it was.

Admiral Keith: We had swimming call, but at the same time, I like to think that when the Cushing sank a year and something later, that some of those men are alive because we tested and found out that if we had wounded people, we'd better get them inside. A man that was able to hang on better stay on the outside, because it would not hold up 24 men. But 24 men could get around it or in it, and you could put men in. Then as they rested, you could put somebody else in. But we stayed in the water long enough to do some real testing.

Q: I've talked to Admiral Parker, who commanded the Cushing when she went down.[*] Quite a dramatic battle.

Admiral Keith: Yes. He wasn't skipper when I was there. We had the Jewish division in my day: O'Brien, Wellings, Jackson, and McInerney.[†] [Laughter]

Q: The Jewish division?

Admiral Keith: All Irishmen.

---

[*] Lieutenant Commander Edward N. Parker, USN, was commanding officer when the Cushing was sunk early on 14 November 1942, during the Naval Battle of Guadalcanal. Vice Admiral Parker has been interviewed as part of the Naval Institute's oral history program.
[†] Destroyer Division Four comprised the Preston (DD-379), Lieutenant Commander Timothy J. O'Brien, USN; the Perkins (DD-377), Lieutenant Commander Timothy F. Wellings, USN; Cushing (DD-376), Lieutenant Commander William B. Jackson, Jr., USN; and the Smith (DD-378), Lieutenant Commander Francis X. McInerney, USN.

* * *

The <u>Cushing</u> was where I first served with Captain Harvey Overesch.[*] He was the division commander, and I was the executive officer and navigator. Whenever he was on the bridge, his tactical officer had to be there, and his tactical officer was me. We were at sea in one stretch for 51 days straight, which was quite an assignment. But I established quite a liking for him, and he for me, and we got along very, very well together wherever we went.

Q: Who was the skipper of the <u>Cushing</u> then?

Admiral Keith: Bill Jackson, who had served in Key West as one of the last people that manned the Key West radio station down there. He was skipper of it, and he became a great friend of Hemingway.[†] He wore a Hemingway mustache, and his mannerisms were quite similar, I'm told, to Hemingway's. But anyhow, that's beside the point.

Q: You also had the internal administration of the ship in addition to those things you've mentioned.

Admiral Keith: Well, I guess I had somebody else do that. [Laughter] As a matter of fact, the previous exec had been relieved about three or four months before I was there, for hitting the bottle too frequently, and Lou Bryan, in '32, the gunnery officer, had served as exec.[‡] So he didn't feel it was necessary to have an exec, that he could handle it. We got along very well.

---

[*] Commander Harvey E. Overesch, USN, was embarked in the <u>Cushing</u> in his role as Commander Destroyer Division Ten. Two years later, as a captain, he was at the Naval Academy when Keith was serving there.
[†] Ernest Hemingway was a celebrated American novelist.
[‡] Lieutenant Louis A. Bryan, USN.

Lou became the exec for Whitey Taylor in the ship that went down.* Lou became a tubercular patient, because that night they went in the water somewhere around 9:00 or 10:00 o'clock, and they were pulled out at daylight or afterwards. He was in the water some seven or eight hours. He found a wounded sailor, an unconscious sailor, and swam with him all night long. The strain that he put on his lungs was attributed to the fact that he subsequently became tubercular and lost his Navy career. He was a cracking good officer.

Whitey Taylor went in the water that night, and he had to swim from the time he went in the water until he was pulled out. He lived in Virginia Beach, and he lived in Hawaii when I was there on duty. I never saw him anywhere near the ocean again in his life. As far as I know, he never went swimming in the ocean again. That's background information, nothing for history, but the fact that you get your ship shot out from under you does have some effect on how you look at things.

Q: Where were you at the time of the attack on Pearl Harbor?

Admiral Keith: I was a duty officer at the United States Naval Academy. In January of 1941 I had received orders to be executive officer of the Cushing, and I went to the Cushing. I thought certainly that I would be there a year or two, but I stayed only five months before I got my orders to the academy. I brought my family from Norfolk all the way out there to Hawaii. They got there in March and went back in June. So you can't outguess them.

The duty at the Naval Academy was something that I had had on my request for duty, and I got it. I went back, and I had a few days' leave at the end of June, then I was due to report in the middle of July. But after ten days or so, I went down to see if I could get quarters. I went to see the secretary of the academic board, Chet Wood, and when I went to his door, Captain Ernest Small was standing at his desk and talking to him.†

---

* Lieutenant Commander Edmund B. Taylor, USN, commanded the USS Duncan (DD-485), which was sunk 12 October 1942 in the Battle of Cape Esperance, on the shore of Guadalcanal.
† Lieutenant Commander Chester C. Wood, USN.

Captain Small at that time was head of the English department at the Naval Academy. Two summers before that, he had been the head of the school ship program in the Drayton for prospective gunnery officers. I was then headed to the Aylwin, and I was assigned to the Drayton to this school. I didn't see a great deal of Captain Small, but when I got to the Aylwin, he was part of the original Hawaiian detachment. I said something earlier about firing on a single drone. Well, Captain Small was the observing division commander when we fired this division practice on these drones.

So I got to the Naval Academy with Captain Small. He turned around, saw me standing at the door, and said, "Oh, there he is now." He had gone over to see Wood. He told him he'd seen my orders to the Naval Academy, and he'd like to have me in his department. I don't mention that to try to boast, but I do use it as indicative that your seniors take a whole lot more notice of the young people that they see growing up behind them than young people ever really realize. Here was a man that I knew, of course, who he was. He had signed a two-month fitness report on me, but that was two years before this thing happened. I was very pleased, but Chip Tisdale, who I said was the operations officer on the Base Force when I was flag lieutenant, had me assigned to the executive department.[*]

Now, when you receive an assignment to the Naval Academy, you don't really know where you want to go. You've never been a teacher or an instructor. But an older friend of mine who was in the fleet in 1941 invited Mrs. Keith and myself to dinner with his wife and his wife at the Halekulani Hotel.[†] He said, "I just wanted to talk to you a little bit about what you want to do when you go back to the Naval Academy."

I said, "Oh, that'll be a nice chance to take a blow. I'd like to teach navigation or teach ordnance and gunnery, something that I've been working in. I think I could be some account in those areas."

He said, "Well, let me talk to you about the Naval Academy. I've been there as an athletic coach, and I've been there as an instructor in a department, and I've had duty in Bancroft Hall as a duty officer. In Bancroft Hall, you have daily contact with the young

---

[*] Captain Tisdale was commandant of midshipmen, 1941-42.
[†] The Halekulani was on Waikiki Beach in Honolulu, Hawaii.

men that are growing up there." It's there that he made a nice comment. He said, "You're the kind of person that I'd like to see influencing the people that are going to follow us on in the Navy. If you have a choice, think a long time about saying you don't want to be a duty officer. There you see midshipmen day by day by day, and if you can send 1 or 101 or 1,001 of them out into the fleet better prepared to do the kind of job that you and I know has got to be done by the officers of the fleet, then you've done the Navy a service that's going to last a long time." So this was in the back of my mind when I found out that I was going to the executive department.

Q: Captain Small was involved in that time in a revision and updating of the ordnance and gunnery textbooks, I think, and fire control.

Admiral Keith: That's right. He went to English from ordnance and gunnery. They were going to put in a naval officer to relieve Carroll S. Alden, who had been 17 years as directing the education of midshipmen in the use of the language. Carroll Alden was the brother-in-law of a superintendent when he got the appointment. I have big ears; I hear a lot that's going on.

Q: What was your specific assignment, then, once you did report to the academy?

Admiral Keith: I did the usual duties of being responsible for the drill instruction of my company, getting people out to do their exercises, tried influencing in Bancroft Hall to bring them up to be military men. We had nothing to do with their education in any of the academic departments; it was their military education that was our responsibility.

Other things that we did were extraneous assignments. We had the war on our hands five months after I got there. The first thing Captain Tisdale, the commandant of midshipmen, said was, "Don't let's go running to Washington, trying to get back to sea. You're not going to leave here until I say you can go, and there's no use going. You've got a job to do here to get these young men ready to go to the fleet. You are sending 500 or 600 out there instead of just one or two a year." The first man to go to sea was Chip

Tisdale. [Laughter] But he was true to his word. He was there when the war started, and he didn't go until April or May, and the rest of us got out in our turn, depending on how long we'd been there. I didn't get out until '43.

One of the things that was taken into consideration in leaving me there till '43 was that it was known that my wife had had a spot on her lung, and she was in a sanitarium. I had twin sons by that time, so the Navy gave me a little extra time before they sent me to sea, although they certainly gave me a wonderful assignment when I went. I got the Nicholas.

We had a system in effect when I went there of assigning aptitude for the service marks. That had been established by Noah, I think, but, anyhow, it wasn't a broad-gauged picture of a midshipman. It was from one company officer, and there were 24 companies there, with maybe some advice from his battalion commander as to what the aptitude for service marks should be. But that was what was assigned. In first class year the multiple for aptitude for the service was the highest of any subject in the curriculum.

Captain Overesch and the executive officer of Bancroft Hall decided that this needed to be changed.[*] I got the job of redesigning and writing up and getting approved a new system, wherein I brought in professors, instructors, naval officers, into various departments, athletic instructors, other people who had an opportunity to see midshipmen outside of Bancroft Hall. I had them put down some sort of evaluation on a chit, turn it in, and then we correlated these chits when we got them. This gave us a broader picture of what we thought of the midshipmen and what their aptitude for the service was. We changed it considerably, and it was well enough received that West Point sent officers down to find out what we were doing, and I was asked to go to West Point and talk to them about it.

Q: Do you have any recollections of the superintendent, Russell Willson?[†]

---

[*] Captain Overesch was commandant of midshipmen, 1942-43.
[†] Rear Admiral Russell Willson, USN, was superintendent of the Naval Academy from February 1941 to January 1942.

Admiral Keith: Yes. Not too much. I knew both of his daughters very well. They were married to good friends of mine.

Q: I've met the one in Florida that's married to Admiral Rice.[*]

Admiral Keith: Yes, Eunice Rice is quite a girl. She was on Porter Road when we were there with Bob Rice. Bob and I had been in PG School together, old friends.

Russell Wilson was ordered out of the Naval Academy the day after Pearl Harbor. He went to Washington and went on the planning staff of Ernie King right away.[†] White House aide John Beardall was ordered to become superintendent, and he stayed there all through the war.[‡] I was very fond of John Beardall and his wife, and I came to know them, although I was a lieutenant commander.

Q: How much contact did you, as a company officer, have with the two superintendents?

Admiral Keith: I'd go to the superintendent's receptions, see him in chapel or something of this kind. It happened that Mrs. Beardall had some reason to know my wife's family, and she went out of her way, as first lady of the Naval Academy, to speak to her. When my wife was ill, she came to see her, and things of this kind. I knew the Beardalls a whole lot better than any other company officer, probably. But that's happenstance. That can happen to anybody that you just happen to know someone.

Q: Are there any of the midshipmen from that era, those 1 or 101, or whatever, that you especially remember?

---

[*] Vice Admiral Robert H. Rice, USN (Ret.), who subsequently died in May 1994.
[†] Admiral Ernest J. King, USN, served as Commander in Chief U.S. Fleet from 20 December 1941 to 2 September 1945.
[‡] Rear Admiral John R. Beardall, USN, was superintendent of the Naval Academy from January 1942 to August 1945.

Admiral Keith: Oh, there are a lot of them that my system picked out. Bill Maxson was an outstanding man in every way at all. He was sent out from the Naval Academy and went to sea, went back to submarine school, then reported to a submarine. One day he was observing from this submarine that was sent out to fire on one of the islands that we were going to invade.* It had a gun on it, and he was up on deck, and shore fire killed him. Ray Peet was selected as a striper under this system.† So was Zumwalt.‡ John Davis is an admiral down the street here.§

The Naval Academy Alumni Association here has a record of inviting all of the candidates from the Naval Academy to a dinner with their families as their guests before they go off to enter the Naval Academy for the first time. I attend these and give them contributions to help them afford to do it. I went when my grandson was going, and the president of the alumni association introduced every one of these 27 midshipmen going from San Diego neighborhood to Annapolis. When he got to R.T.S. Keith, and he said, "R.T.S. Keith. I know that name. I, in fact, see your grandfather here tonight. He was my company officer when I was a midshipman. And I want to tell you, young man, that he wielded a sharp sword." He shook his finger at him and said, "But it was always fair."**

So there's another one that we pulled out of the list and pointed the finger at as being good material. I don't know, but there were just a lot of them that, even in those days, they were outstanding among their peers. I think that a good aptitude system helps you identify these people.

*   *   *

When the war came along, they began to place Naval Reserve units in various colleges all around the country. They put military and naval officers there, and they trained

---

* Lieutenant (junior grade) Willis E. Maxson III, USN, was in the class of 1943. He was killed in October 1943 on board the submarine Skate (SS-305).
† Midshipman Raymond E. Peet, USN, class of 1943, eventually retired as a four-star admiral.
‡ Midshipman Elmo R. Zumwalt, Jr., USN, class of 1943, became a four-star admiral and served as CNO, 1970-74.
§ Midshipman John B. Davis, Jr., USN, who stood high in the class of 1942, retired as a rear admiral.
** Robert Taylor Scott Keith III graduated from the Naval Academy in the class of 1987.

the students, graduated them, and gave them commissions in the Navy after certain quick training following their college years.

Someone called the superintendent's office at the Naval Academy and said that St. John's had cadet barracks from when it used to be a military school.* These barracks were practically empty, so St. John's wanted to get a Naval Reserve unit there so that they could fill up their ranks a little bit during the war. We called the dean out there. I was given the job by the commandant to head a group that included a number of CEC officers who were to make studies of the buildings, as to whether they were adequate.† A supply officer also went with me; he was supposed to determine whether we could feed people there, things of this kind. I went to look at the barracks and see if we could house them adequately. One of the civilian professors went along to talk to St. John's about studies, whether they would cover the ground that they needed, to give them preparation that they needed to go into the Navy. We came back and made a report. It seemed that St. John's could have a unit of umpteen people; I've forgotten what the numbers were.

Shortly after that, Winky Barr, who was the head of the great books program at St. John's, got hold of everybody in Congress that he knew from Maryland, and he started blowing his stack all over the place.‡ I'd never seen him. I'd just made a survey that the dean had said was all right. The Navy thought that they had been asked by St. John's to do this. Winky Barr was enraged that the Navy had always tried to take over St. John's, and that they wanted the land out there, and this was the first move to take over St. John's. He called every graduate of St. John's from the year of 1696, when it was founded, to rise up and spin in his grave against the Naval Academy for doing this heinous crime.

So Admiral Beardall, the superintendent, called me and said, "What's this all about?"

I said, "I don't know, sir."

He said, "Well, Admiral Denfeld's got to send somebody up to Congress, and he wants us to send somebody. You're it."§ So I went to Washington to find out what this

---

* St. John's College is across the street from the Naval Academy in Annapolis, Maryland.
† CEC--Civil Engineer Corps.
‡ Dr. Stringfellow Barr served as president of St. John's College from 1937 to 1946.
§ Rear Admiral Louis E. Denfeld, USN, was Assistant Chief of Naval Personnel.

was. Here was my old squadron commander from the <u>Aylwin</u> days, Louie Denfeld.* He asked me, "Taylor, what in the world are you doing down in Annapolis?" [Laughter] So we had quite a merry-go-round about this.

He sent me off to go up before a Senate committee. Before I went up, he said, "Tell them we don't want St. John's. We thought St. John's was anxious to put in a Naval Reserve unit." So I made a spiel and so forth, but I had three senators--Senator Saltonstall, Senator Byrd, and Senator Macmahon or someone about that name from Oklahoma or Nevada; I don't remember where.† Those three gentlemen sat down and listened and asked me questions. This began my feeling, which was furthered during my three years here in Washington in '46 to '49, that if you had an opportunity to sit down and talk to Congress, and set the facts before them, that the Congress would come up with a pretty darn good solution to the problem.

Q: What was the outcome of the case involving St. John's?

Admiral Keith: Just what you'd expect it to be--that the Navy said, "We have no designs on St. John's. We have no reason to think that we should take over St. John's, and we were not properly advised, in that we thought that St. John's would like to fill their empty buildings." I had facts and figures as to how many people actually lived in them, and what their capacities for the buildings were at St. John's, how many students they had, and they had less than 100 students. So that there was plenty of room, and most people were very anxious to get the Naval Reserve.

Anyhow, the experience of appearing before Congress, of having to defend your position, is, I think, part of growing up in the Navy, because they come into the lifeblood of the Navy, appropriations, and so many things, so often.

*   *   *

---

* As a captain, Denfeld had served a tour as Commander Destroyer Squadron One from June 1940 to January 1941.
† Senator Leverett Saltonstall (Republican-Massachusetts); Senator Harry F. Byrd (Democrat-Virginia); the third was probably Senator Patrick McCarran (Democrat-Nevada).

I left the Naval Academy after that first tour and was fortunate to get command of the Nicholas, a ship that was one of the first of the modern 2,100-ton destroyers to report to Admiral Halsey when he was down to the South Pacific, fighting that battle for Guadalcanal.* The Nicholas was lucky that it went through the war without serious damage. It had one overhaul of about four weeks in the States, while I was skipper of it, and that's the only one she had from when she reported in '42 until the war was over. I think she got home before '46 came in. I had a wonderful crew on there. They all knew their jobs.

The ship won a Presidential Unit Citation for a battle in the Solomons before I was captain of her.† I was the captain that received the citation when we got to Pearl Harbor in 1944, January. Admiral Nimitz and Admiral Kauffman, who was Commander Destroyer Force, presented us, made a very fine talk, which I have a copy of.‡ Admiral Nimitz praised the Nicholas's fighting, and she fought all through Guadalcanal.

I relieved just after Tarawa and went back to the yard.§ Then I went back and fought the war in General MacArthur's Navy in the Southwest Pacific. But when I first got out to the southwest, Halsey was still there, so I went to several of his morning conferences when we were down in Noumea on an R&R.** That's where I got to know Admiral Carney and met Admiral Halsey.†† Admiral Felix Johnson was down there.‡‡ He was secretary of the academic board when I was on duty at the Naval Academy my first tour.

---

* USS Nicholas (DD-449) was commissioned 4 June 1942. She had a standard displacement of 2,050 tons, was 376 feet long, and 40 feet in the beam. Her top speed was 37 knots. She was armed with five 5-inch guns, ten 40-millimeter guns, and ten 21-inch torpedo tubes.
† The Nicholas was flagship for the Battle of Kolombangara on 12-13 July 1943. Her commanding officer then was Lieutenant Commander Andrew J. Hill, USN.
‡ Admiral Chester W. Nimitz, USN; Rear Admiral James R. Kauffman, USN.
§ The invasion of Tarawa in the Gilbert Islands was in November 1943. She arrived at San Francisco on 15 December to begin her overhaul.
** R&R--rest and recreation.
†† Rear Admiral Robert B. Carney, USN, was chief of staff to Admiral William F. Halsey, USN, Commander South Pacific Force.
‡‡ Captain Felix L. Johnson, USN, served from November 1943 to June 1944 as assistant chief of staff to Commander South Pacific Force, Admiral Halsey. The oral history of Johnson, who retired as a vice admiral, is in the Naval Institute collection.

* * *

One thing that had always puzzled me, when I was getting ready to fight the Nicholas, was that there were so many times that destroyers were illuminated by Japanese big-ship searchlights, and they were blinding. When a searchlight is so big that it blinds a destroyer, you know darn well it's not coming from another destroyer; they just don't have that much illumination. So you can figure you're outgunned, and you'd better try to do something to get rid of that light so that you can go hide somewhere. So I figured that they were big and long, and the searchlights were pretty well out, and I put in plan four.

We had three different conditions of gun readiness. Mine was to take all the horizontal parallax out of the computer or the director, and just have all the 5-inch guns point straight out, so that they covered as much horizontal as they possibly could. Then we'd cut the fuzes--so that the projectiles would burst before they got to the range we had that target at--and just let fly, to see if some of these shrapnel things would knock that searchlight out for us. We never had to use it, but at least we were beginning to think ahead and see what we could find out to try and do.

* * *

Captain Noble was in command of an amphibious group in the South Pacific when we went in to Aitape.[*] I was in support and hadn't fired a shot all day. He hadn't needed any. We didn't have very much difficulty in Aitape.

He finally sent me a message that said, "There's an island over here that looks a little suspicious to me. Wish you'd go over and see if you can stir up a little fire over there. I think they've got something stored."

So I steamed over, took up position, and let go. Sure enough, I hit some oil drums or something, because I started a fire. I was firing away, and finally he said, "I don't want you to try to knock the island out of the water; just let up now." [Laughter] But, you see, in those days, you'd go back to some association.[†] He knew who he was giving that order

---

[*] On 22 April 1944 the Nicholas covered the Aitape landings on the north coast of New Guinea. Captain Albert G. Noble, USN, was in command of Task Group 77.3, the eastern attack group.

[†] They got to know each before the war, when Keith was on the Base Force staff and Noble was on the CinCUS staff.

to. He knew I'd been itching to shoot all day long, and he gave me a chance to shoot, and then he sent me a sassy message that said, "I didn't tell you to try to blow the island out of the water."

* * *

The <u>Nicholas</u> had great competence. The men did their jobs extremely well. We took advantage of every bit of training that we had, the time that we had to improve what we had to do. Our gunnery was excellent. We wanted to show off. After MacArthur took the Admiralty Islands, we anchored destroyers off the island where the First Cavalry Division was located.[*] I met General Swift at the club there.[†] MacArthur didn't allow any liquor in the forward areas, but the Navy did. So the destroyers were given a Quonset hut and established a club over there, which the Army was delighted to have on board the island. When we were in port, we would journey over there and have a libation before turning in at night, and tell a lot of lies about what great heroes we'd been. One night I was talking to General Swift. I said, "We're going out tomorrow morning to shoot an antiaircraft practice outside the harbor. Would you like to go out and see it?"

He said, "I certainly would."

So I sent a boat over for him. Before he left, I said, "Maybe you'd like to bring some of your men along." So he brought about 20 soldiers with him. When they came aboard, I asked them if they'd had breakfast.

They said, "Oh, yes, we've had breakfast."

I said, "Did you have eggs for breakfast this morning?"

They said, "We haven't seen an egg for two months, three months."

So I said, "Well, go on down. We just got alongside a supply ship, and we've got a lot of eggs." Not a one of those soldiers ever saw a gun shoot; they stayed there and ate the whole time they were on board! [Laughter] But they had a good time.

* * *

We picked up two Japanese submarines. Our submarine policy on the <u>Nicholas</u> in my day was that unless we were protecting someone, then we would not make urgent depth

---

[*] General Douglas MacArthur, USA, Commander Southwest Pacific Force.
[†] Major General Innis P. Swift, USA, commander of the First Cavalry Division.

charge attacks, because they disturbed the water so much that it was hard to regain contact and to make a deliberate attack. Both submarines that we had, we got well away from the ship on radar, and then got a sound contact subsequently.

We were in Hollandia one day when I got orders to go with the Taylor to Ulithi. We were to meet the St. Louis, which was rejoining the fleet from battle damage and was assigned to the Southwest Pacific Navy, and escort her from Ulithi to Kossol Roads. We sailed somewhere around sunset from Ulithi.

Q: When was this?

Admiral Keith: This would be November of '44.[*] Somewhere around 8:00 o'clock in the evening, the Nicholas picked up a radar contact, and our SG radar really was well-operated.[†] They got this contact at over 21,000, 22,000 yards. We closed, and we found that we had a disappearing contact. We went in and got sonar contact. About 8:30, we dropped one depth charge pattern. We continued to pick up intermittently an echo on our sonar, and we never could get him dead to rights, get a good lead on him. We figured afterwards that we had damaged this sub in our first attack, when we had rolled or thrown 18 or so depth charges at him. He was probably using the disturbed water from that first attack to try to sneak away from us. A depth charge does leave roiled water around, which you couldn't range through. But we were so clever that he couldn't get away, so we were patting ourselves on the back.

About two hours later, we got a contact, and we had him pretty well dead to rights and had a good lead on him, which you had to take in those days to drop. As we went in, we had a left lead. We got to about 175 yards, which is about the shortest range you could get, and you were committed when you got there. Then my sonar officer said, "Captain, that bastard is going right as hard as he can." We spun the wheel right, backed on our starboard engine, and let go with depth charges, because we were practically right over him then. Sure enough, several minutes later, after the last depth charge had gone off--how

---

[*] The incident described here took place on 12 November 1944.
[†] The SG was a surface-search radar.

many minutes, I can't say now; it's in my battle report--we got one of the durnedest underwater explosions you ever heard. I was standing on the pelorus, watching to see when to make my next turn to try and regain contact, and I was almost lifted off my feet up in the air. I couldn't have been lifted off my feet, because some damage would have been done to the hull, but none was. But it was a terrific explosion, and you could feel it. It lifted the ship somewhat.

Immediately the St. Louis and the Taylor, which had withdrawn to the south of me, called me and said, "Are you all right?" They could feel it that quickly, the concussion through the water, 25 miles away from me by this time. So it was quite an explosion.

Well, after the war, we found out that we had sunk the Japanese I-37. Until this year, I thought that we had damaged him and that he had been trying to escape us all this time. One of my young sailormen on the Nicholas, that I saw at a reunion down at Jackson, Mississippi, asked me if I'd read a book called Suicide Torpedo, Suicide Submarine. I said I'd never seen it. So he sent it to me. He said, "You'll be interested in it, because it talks about the I-37 being sunk by us, and it was one of the carriers of the suicide torpedoes."[*]

This young Japanese tells about being recruited into the secret weapon system that was going to win the war for the Emperor in June of 1944. They carry him across Japan and out into one of the outlying southern islands, and he goes down, gets there at night. The next morning he goes down, and he sees this great Long Lance torpedo, with a compartment on it and with a periscope on it. He says, "Oh. I'm going to ride a suicide torpedo." That's what they told him: that they were going to carry him in and give him a steer for his target, and he was going to then be able to go and deliver a 3,000-pound warhead and destroy anything that it hits, big enough to really blow them out of the water--100 hits, and 100 ships would be sunk.

So then he goes on to say that they put these torpedoes on the first three Japanese submarines, and they carried four of them. They had four hatches connecting the torpedoes to the steerers' compartment on the torpedo, and they had four cables on to hold them

---

[*] Yukuta Yokota, with Joseph D. Harrington was the author of The Kaiten Weapon (New York: Ballantine Books, 1962). Page 46 tells of the I-37 being sunk by the Nicholas. U.S. sources identify the victim as the I-38.

down. They sent out the first three of them, two of them to go to Ulithi, and one of them to go to Kossol Roads. He said, "My friends that were in the one headed for Kossol Roads were unfortunate. They met the USS Nicholas and never came back." It was in there, four young men with their swords in their hands, a picture taken before they went out to ride these torpedoes, and that's the first time I've ever seen anybody that I killed. So it was a new experience.

One of the others went to Ulithi, and it was the one that sank the Mississinewa, and the other one got in an attack on a smaller vessel and damaged it; it didn't sink.[*] The Japanese story in that fits in with what we have recorded in the war in the Pacific from our friend Morison.

Q: Well, that's one thing about naval warfare--it's not as personal as the warfare on land. You very seldom do see the people.

Admiral Keith: It was a different expression to see four nice 17-, 18-year-old boys, 19 years old, that were your victims.

Before I had believed that that fellow was damaged. After reading this book, I realized that it was the responsibility of the captain of the submarine to get his submarine in position so that this guy in the torpedo could steer from that position. He would get it into initial course so many thousand yards, and then at a certain point, he put up his periscope and homed in directly on the target. This was after having been positioned and giving the initial steer and the last contact with the Japanese sub as his steer to the target.

So now that I look at it, I think that we were fighting a battle with this sub skipper this whole time. He was trying to get into position so that he had enough distance from me to launch his suicide torpedo and to give it a steer. But with me continually circling him, and him using the waters to get away from me, he never could get distance enough away from me to launch his torpedoes. I think the terrific underwater explosion now came from those torpedoes in some manner being set off by our depth charges, and that they sank a

---

[*] On 20 November a Japanese kaiten suicide torpedo sank the fleet oiler Mississinewa ((AO-59) at Ulithi Atoll in the Caroline Islands.

little bit lower, and then they blew. So it gives you quite a different visualization of your encounter than the one that you visualized from such knowledge as you had without any knowledge from the other side.

Q: And you didn't realize that your tenacity on staying after him had so much to do with your self-preservation.

Admiral Keith: I never thought that I was in any real danger. I thought he was the one at first. I thought I was on search-and-destroy, and this duel idea is something I think about now in the peace of my home.

*   *   *

I have written and I have talked about the men who make up a ship: the people who, in time of battle, can hear the guns going off, but their job is in the engine room; their job is in the radio shack; their job is down in the bowels of the ship somewhere. All they know is that they've got this job in front of them, and if they don't do it, then the people up there that are fighting the ship probably won't get to the point where they should be in order to fight. But they can't see what's going on.

I had a wartime officer of the deck who is now a professor at the University of Wisconsin, and I had a helmsman who was my general quarters helmsman. They had to stay in under the bridge when the kamikazes were coming down. All they could do was stand there at the end of the telephones and hear what my talker was telling them to do. The officer would repeat it, and the helmsman would carry it out. But they didn't come running out to see why we were huddled down and hoping that kamikaze wasn't going to hit us. They stayed by their jobs. It's just so essential that we recognize the great contributions made by every man in the ship, and how important it is that the pieces fit together in order for a ship to fight.

*   *   *

I went back to commission the Herbert J. Thomas at Bath, Maine, in the spring of 1945.[*] Having left the Nicholas in January of '45, I was able to go and talk to the family of one of her radar maintenance men who came from Bath. I told them that we were alive, I felt, because of the genius of their son in maintaining the SG radar. He had never been to a school, but he just lived inside of that thing, and he knew every tube, he knew every wire, he knew everything that was in it. When something went wrong, he could find it. It would go down at night, and you'd wake up the next morning, and there it was working again. I was able to talk to his family about it.

When V-E Day came, we were still in Bath, and they were very much afraid that they would just pull out and say, "Well, the war's over, as far as we're concerned. Stop building ships."[†] So with the war going on, they wanted us to talk about it to the workers and see if we could get through and keep the ships on the schedule of one a week being delivered from Bath, which it was at that time. I told them about the war, standing up and talking about their sons to these men and women who were making the ships in Bath. I told them what I thought of this radar maintenance man's competencies and how long he worked and how hard he fought for them. Bath didn't lose any time. But things like that, that you can see a man and cite him, it makes a lot of difference when you're talking to people who know him.

When I took command of the Herbert J. Thomas, we were in the midst of getting all sorts of reports of battle damage in the spring, when the kamikazes were really getting going good off Okinawa. I'd just come back from seeing the kamikazes get started in the fall of '44. It was bad enough when we had 30 or 40 of them coming in, but they were up to hundreds of them by the time I'm talking about.

---

[*] USS Herbert J. Thomas (DD-833) was a Gearing-class destroyer built at the Bath Iron Works and commissioned 29 May 1945. She had a standard displacement of 2,400 tons, was 390 feet long, and 41 feet in the beam. Her top speed was 35 knots. She was armed with six 5-inch guns, 14 40-millimeter and 16 20-millimeter guns, and ten 21-inch torpedo tubes.

[†] V-E Day--Victory in Europe Day, 8 May 1945, when the German surrender was ratified in Berlin.

I sent my chief engineer and damage control officer down to the Bureau of Ships in Washington. They stayed down there two weeks on temporary duty, studying battle damage to ships that had been reported, so that they could come back and write battle problems, predicated on actual damage that had been suffered, and what holes were made, what lines were cut, and everything else.

A little later, when I was desdiv commander in the Turner, we had some of the damndest battle problems.* We'd take out one thing and just do one place at a time, to train the damage control parties.

*   *   *

The interest of visitors in Navy ships is remarkable. They love to come. My most impressive title in all my life in the Navy was commander of visiting ships, Nimitz Day, Washington, D.C., October of 1945. When Nimitz came back to become CNO, Washington turned itself inside out.† I was up in Maine in my destroyer division flagship, which was a radar picket ship that was going through refresher training at Guantanamo when the war was over. There was nothing for us to do, but you know that they converted 24 destroyers after the kamikazes became such a threat, to make them radar picket ships with a lot more capability to handle the raids.

Q: Admiral Willis Lee was doing some research up at Casco Bay.‡

Admiral Keith: That's right. We weren't in Casco Bay. We were in another anchorage in Maine, and I can't remember the name of it. It was too long ago. But I got orders to go down and be the boss of visiting ships in Washington. They told me to get there on Wednesday morning. I asked them if it would be all right for me to go down and get in on

---

* When Keith became Commander Destroyer Division 17, his flagship was the USS Turner (DD-834), a sister of the Herbert J. Thomas.
† Fleet Admiral Chester Nimitz, USN, served as Chief of Naval Operations from 15 December 1945 to 15 December 1947. The Nimitz Day celebration in Washington, including a parade and speech to Congress, was on 5 October.
‡ Vice Admiral Willis A. Lee, Jr., had spent July and August doing experimental work in Casco Bay, Maine, in an effort to find an effective means of dealing with kamikazes. Lee died 25 August 1945, shortly after the Japanese ceased hostilities.

Tuesday night. I said I didn't want to transit the river, unless necessary, at night. So they said all right. That was excuse enough. I went down at 30 knots from Maine in the <u>Turner</u>. We went into Washington and tied up, and we had LSTs, and we had an LCI, and very small ships. I got them all together, and we found out what sort of equipment we had on board, because we expected there would be a lot more visitors than the small ships could handle at one time and that there would be lines on the dock.

So we arranged for each ship to put on the dock various types of fire-fighting equipment. We had handy billies that we got a periodic stream from to show them how that worked, and how you could get water out of the sea.[*] We showed them diving equipment. We put divers over the side. We showed them anything we could think of in the way of rescue breathing apparatuses, anything else in your damage control parties. Along with the equipment we had picked men that would smile and tell the stories nicely. It was very, very well received--that we had something for people to do, rather than stand and twiddle their thumbs in line until they could get on board ship.

* * *

When I was in Washington in the facilities game in '46 to '49, my primary duty was the redistribution and disposal of surplus property from World War II BuPers activities.[†] We had laundry equipment, we had school equipment, desks, chairs, blackboards. We had houses, and lots of housing was built around wartime facilities that was surplus when the war was over. In my office I had Rita Lenihan, who I see you have the history of.[‡] She can tell you a lot about it, because she did a lot of the spade work, of reviewing these houses.

We had a CEC officer, a commander, there. He found out what these houses were built of, whether or not they had any life expectancy that would serve us that well. We must have reviewed 30,000 different housing units in groups. We finally came up with a request for so many houses, of which we got about 13,000 houses scattered around the United States, in которых we put our personnel granted for temporary duty.

---

[*] Handy billy is the designation of a small portable pump.
[†] BuPers--Bureau of Naval Personnel.
[‡] Lieutenant Rita Lenihan, USN, was one of the early women naval officers. Her oral history is in the Naval Institute collection.

At the same time, we were building Naval Reserve training armories all over the place. Before I got there, the Navy people were smart in that they said, "We don't want to make any permanent construction. We want to take some of these surplus Quonset huts and make them into armories, where we can maintain the skills of the naval reservists and be available if we ever need them."* The Congress bought that. The Army and the Air Force never got a thing, and we got appropriations year after year after year for building up the reserves in these temporary armories. The temporary armories are still around in a lot of cases--one of them right down here.

Q: The idea being that that wouldn't cost as much as a permanent installation?

Admiral Keith: Oh, we didn't say. We just wanted money to erect them. When we erected them, we put a facade on the front of them, and we did a lot of plumbing work and things, put them on concrete blocks. You just couldn't put a Quonset hut up in most towns; they would protest it. A lot of people protested it even with the facade we put on them. We had to put facades on both ends of some, to make them dressed up. But we were able to find ways to do it, and we built a lot of reserve armories. I think the Navy has certainly reaped a great harvest from the reserves. Without the reserves, we couldn't have flown to the Berlin Wall; without the reserves, we couldn't have fought the Korean War; we couldn't have fought the war in Vietnam, because they filled the holes in the ranks. I can't say too much about my experiences with the reserves. But, there again, I had the chance to expand my views by having different things to look at and to deal with.

When I was there, since I was in the facilities, they wanted a BuPers representative on a board appointed to study the future needs of the Naval Academy, to draw up a major plan for development there. I was a member of Admiral Ben Moreell's committee.† We had

---

* A Quonset hut is a semi-cylindrical metal building that can be shipped to an advance base area and erected quickly.
† Admiral Ben Moreell, CEC, USN (Ret.), had been Chief of the Bureau of Yards and Docks throughout World War II. In December 1941 he founded the Naval Construction Battalions, better known as the Seabees.

Holabird and Root, that great design and architectural firm in Chicago.[*] Root was a very interesting man, who did his best to decide how the land around the Naval Academy could be utilized to best advantage, what the possibilities were.[†]

I think we recommended that they take over those three blocks right outside the gate, that runs down by the old Peggy Stewart Inn and the Cooper Apartments, and down to the wall, where you go in off of St. John's campus--but not St. John's. They filled in up around the boathouse. Well, the filling in was changed to filling in down where the tennis courts and the boat basin used to be, and to extend the land out in that direction. Most of the buildings built in subsequent years--the science buildings, the libraries, and the assembly halls, and things of this kind--were all part of Ben Morrell's plan when he submitted it.[‡]

To go there today and see what they've built, and to look back to 1946-47, when this study was made, it's just remarkable how competent those people were--there was very little I could do. When they started talking about the facilities underground and what was going to be needed there, it was over my head. But that was right up Holabird and Root's and Ben Morrell's line. When they started talking about what science buildings and things they needed, they had experts from MIT and other places to advise them, and they came up with a Jim Dandy good report.[§] So, there again, you have an opportunity to see and learn a little.

Another thing that I served on during those three years was the board headed by the three assistant secretaries of the services. John Nicholas Brown was the Assistant Secretary of the Navy; C. V. Whitney was the Assistant Secretary of the Air Force; and Gordon Gray was the Assistant Secretary of the Army. The study that was given them, that they spent a good many months working on, was whether or not the National Guard should be federalized. I was there more or less because the Naval Reserve was a federal unit, and the National Guard was not, and therefore, the Air National Guard was not.

---

[*] Holabird & Root & Burges, Architects and Engineers.
[†] John Wellborn Root was a member of the special advisory commission.
[‡] The commission's detailed report was dated 28 December 1948. A copy is on file in a folder titled "Buildings and Grounds Expansion of the Naval Academy," in the Naval Academy archives.
[§] MIT--Massachusetts Institute of Technology.

These secretaries and their chief military men on the boards finally came up with a report that said that the National Guard should be federalized. It was a magnificent report. The senior Army man, who signed the report, was a major general or a lieutenant general. He had come right out of the National Guard and had been commissioned in the regular Army, and then stayed in the Army after the war. So he was persona non grata with the National Guard from the beginning. That report should have been approved, and certainly the commanders in the National Guard had never proven out in time of war. They nearly all had to be replaced, and there were plenty of people down the line in the National Guard who, if promotion has been on an aptitude system, would have proven their abilities early. But there were too many politics involved in the generals that came up at state level.

Many, many years later, after I was retired, I met Gordon Gray again. I had a chance to talk to him, and I asked him why he thought that it had failed. It was like what I told you earlier about everybody that had ever been at St. John's rising up and protesting the Navy taking over St. John's. He said, "Every governor of every state that ever existed rose up in his grave and protested the taking away of this great and good guard from the states." They had beautiful houses at some forts that were made available to the governors. The governor of Virginia has the most beautiful house down in Virginia Beach you ever saw, down at Fort Pendleton--which is an old abandoned fort that never lost its National Guard. You drive down Ocean Boulevard in Virginia Beach, and you come to Atlantic Boulevard, and you come to it.

Anyhow, Gordon Gray said that the governors had too many perquisites involved, with an airplane from the Air National Guard at their disposal during times of peace, to fly them around the state, and the perquisites of having the military escort and things of this kind that governors get from the guard. The head of the National Guard is always on the governor's staff. It was too much. We couldn't beat that and get them federalized, where the federal government would control them and not the governor. So there again, you see, decision-making sometimes becomes political. You wonder how we've done as well as we have, as we've gone through over 200 years in this country.

*   *   *

As you can see from the record, I had duty at the Naval Academy subsequent to this. When I was secretary of the academic board, I went to Washington, and I asked that people of certain qualifications be assigned to the Naval Academy. We had a hard time ever getting good fighter pilots, or outstanding naval aviators, to come to the Naval Academy for duty. They didn't want it. They would go anywhere rather than do that, because there was no way that they could keep their flying status and their hand in flying the kind of planes that they were used to and that they wanted to fly. A fighter didn't want to go down and fly one of those little things that sat on the water at the Naval Academy in those days. But we talked to the chief of BuAer, and we told him that it was in his interest in the future to get more of the top-flight midshipmen interested in aviation, and that he should take that into consideration in the kind of officers he sent to duty down there.[*] We got some pretty top-flight people eventually.

It was my duty, once officers were assigned to the Naval Academy, to put them in the seamanship department, the electrical engineering, ordnance and gunnery, wherever it was. I don't think you could find one of them that I ever talked to that won't tell you that he heard the Keith pitch that I told you I was given years earlier in Honolulu: "If you can send 1 or 1,001 to sea better prepared because of their contact with you to do the kinds of job that you, from your experience in the fleet, know those young officers have got to do, then you've done a great service to your country and the Navy." That's a carryover, and I still feel that way about your chances, when you are instructing youth.

*   *   *

---

[*] Rear Admiral Alfred M. Pride, USN, served as Chief of the Bureau of Aeronautics from 1 May 1947 to 1 May 1951. Rear Admiral Thomas S. Combs, USN, held the post from 1 May 1951 to 30 June 1953.

Back in the '20s, when I first went to the Naval Academy, I didn't know that I wanted to be a naval officer. I didn't realize then what the proper answer is. But when I was secretary of the academic board years later, I was asked a question by a candidate in the days when the Secretary of the Navy first had the ability to appoint people from the qualified alternates list. In those days, he could send about 60, 80, or 100 qualified people to the Naval Academy on Secretary of the Navy appointments. A young man said to me, "I'm not sure that I want to be a naval officer, and I think it would be unfair to take one of these appointments away from someone who wants it but is only an alternate and can't get an appointment. I think it would be wrong for me to do it."

I said, "I've thought of this a good deal. But the truth of the matter is that very few young men, no matter what line of endeavor academically they are pursuing, really know what they want to be. Look at the number of lawyers who are bankers, the numbers of doctors who don't practice their profession. The people who know what they're going to do are probably sons that are going to follow in their fathers' footsteps. It would be unfair if you took a free and magnificent education from the Navy, knowing that you were going to use that education in your father's business or do something else as soon as you could. That would be wrong. But once you graduate and go out and give the Navy an opportunity, which is all that they are entitled to, that is the Navy's opportunity to prove to you that being a naval officer is, to you, a satisfying and satisfactory life. In other words, that you go out into the fleet with an open mind is all that's required, and that's all that could be hoped for."

*   *   *

We have an honor system at the Naval Academy now, instead of an aptitude system. Admiral Hill was very anxious to overcome a tradition of the Naval Academy classes that you never reported a classmate.[*] Now, this had been handed down and handed down and handed down, no matter what they did. You could see a man cheat, you could see a man lie, steal, and you still, if he were your classmate, didn't do anything about it.

---

[*] Vice Admiral Harry W. Hill, USN, was superintendent of the Naval Academy from April 1950 to August 1952.

The idea that Admiral Hill had was that an honor system says you can't lie, you can't steal, and you can't cheat and be a proper candidate to be a commissioned officer in the Navy. There shouldn't be any exceptions where classmates overlooked these offenses. If they believed that an offense is one that is unbecoming to and unfitting for a wearer of the uniform of an officer of the Navy, then they should make up their minds about it right now as midshipmen, because if a man gets orders from the captain to do such and such on his watch, and he forgets to do it, then lies about it, the whole ship can be jeopardized. If you can't trust your shipmates with your valuables, if they steal from you, they're not shipmates. If they lie, steal, cheat, if they falsify papers to their advantage when they're officers, responsible for making reports, the Navy's going to suffer. There's just too many examples of why a liar or a cheat or a thief doesn't belong in the military officer's uniform.

So he asked the classes to consider his views, to consider their thoughts, and after they had had plenty of time to discuss it, to have that class's view presented to him, as to whether they were going to adopt this standard in that class. He said that he would hold nothing against them if they wanted to abide by a tradition that was wrong, in his opinion. He recognized it, he had known of its existence, but he became superintendent, and he wanted to do something about it. He waited for an opportunity where he had enthusiasm in the brigade. That came when they unexpectedly won a football game, 14 to 2, from Army in 1950. I remember a telegram coming from an air base in Morocco or somewhere in that area, saying, "Quatorze a deux! Quatorze a deux! That is the way it ought to work." There was a rather loud rally after the game and victory.

So the various classes all discussed it, and they all talked about their feelings about this. They finally said, "We agree." If you ask Bill Lawrence about this--he was president of the first class when it happened, and he was also president of the brigade honor committee--I think that his class, as first class, led the way in saying, "We concur."[*]

I've been told--not by Bill himself--but I've been told that Bill Lawrence stated that having to stand up before his class and argue with the people who didn't agree with Admiral

---

[*] Midshipman William P. Lawrence, USN, was president of the Naval Academy's class of 1951. While being interviewed as part of the Naval Institute's oral history program, he spent considerable time discussing the development of the Naval Academy honor concept.

Hill's position, and defend Admiral Hill's position, and defend the Navy's position, and then having to go before the other classes, who had asked for him to come down and talk to them along the same lines, and having to again argue a point, defend a point, gave him a sense of the meaning of things that stood him as well as anything in his past did, when he was a prisoner of war. If you talk to him some time, you might bring this subject up to see if he says it.

Q: I'd like to do that.[*]

*   *   *

I have a story that I'm going to send to David Eisenhower, because I'm reading his book now about his grandfather.[†]

This goes back to my days as secretary of the academic board at the Naval Academy, to begin with. In those days, the Navy and Princeton, Navy and Columbia, Navy and Pennsylvania--all played football games. All those schools found out that having some of the midshipmen march on the field before the game helped their attendance sufficiently for them to pay half of the expenses to go to those games. The athletic association took the members of the athletic association board of control to the games as their guests. I was the superintendent's representative on the athletic committee.

We went to New York. General Eisenhower was president of Columbia University, and Admiral Hill, a distinguished amphibian commander during the war, was the superintendent of the Naval Academy.[‡] An invitation arrived from the Columbia Athletic Association, asking Admiral Hill to luncheon before the Columbia game, in their boathouse right next to the stadium where we played. Admiral Hill felt that because of the military juxtaposition of the two heads of the two schools, that the niceties of the situation required that the president of Columbia invite him as superintendent of the Naval Academy. But the

---

[*] In his oral history Admiral Lawrence said that the Naval Academy graduates provided the strongest core of leadership in the Vietnamese prisoner of war camps.
[†] David Eisenhower is the grandson of President Dwight D. Eisenhower.
[‡] From 1948 to 1950, between stints of active duty in the Army, Eisenhower was president of Columbia University in New York City.

invitation wasn't from Eisenhower, so Admiral Hill declined, and had, I guess, somewhat hurt feelings.

It was unknown to him at the time that Eisenhower said he wouldn't be able to attend the Columbia game. However, on the day of the game, we were all assembled, having a pre-luncheon drink at the boathouse at Columbia. The door opened, and Eisenhower walked in. He'd just come back from Washington from several days of conferring down there. It came out later that he had just been told that he was going to head up the formation of the NATO Supreme Headquarters in Paris.[*] We didn't know that at this time.

Just as Eisenhower came in, they came in to say that the midshipmen were all arrived and ready to march on the field. The senior Naval Academy representative there was Captain Bob Pirie, commandant of midshipmen, and the next senior was Taylor Keith.[†] So Captain Pirie had to go out because there were midshipmen going to march onto the field, and he had to stand and receive their salute. So he was out. I don't know whether he got a sandwich or not. Anyhow, that ended up with me sitting on General Eisenhower's right at luncheon. It was a very interesting occasion for me. But what I want to tell you about it is his turning to me at luncheon and saying, "Captain, did you ever know Swede Hazlett in the Navy?"

You shake your head. Have I told you this story?

Q: No, sir, but he worked with Admiral Davidson in the Bureau of Navigation, and Davidson told me that he was a very close friend of Eisenhower's from Kansas.[‡]

Admiral Keith: Well, let me finish my story. Don't you tell it for me.

---

[*] In December 1950 Eisenhower returned to active duty to head up the military command for the North Atlantic Treaty Organization, which had been founded the year before.
[†] Captain Robert B. Pirie, USN, served from 1949 to 1952 as the Naval Academy's commandant of midshipmen. His oral history is in the Naval Institute collection.
[‡] Edward E. Hazlett, Jr., graduated from the Naval Academy in 1915, the same year his boyhood friend Dwight Eisenhower graduated from West Point. For health reasons he retired from active duty on 1 January 1939 in the rank of captain.

Eisenhower said, "Do you know Swede Hazlett?"

I said, "Well, sir, I know him, but I can't say that I know him well."

He said, "Oh, he had one of the finest minds I've ever known in my life. He was the clearest thinker. One of the greatest tragedies of World War II is when he had a heart attack and had to be retired by the Navy. But when I was Chief of Staff in Washington after the war, and when the muddle of Washington got me all muddled up in my thinking, I'd take a day off and go down to North Carolina and sit on the side of a hill with Swede and talk.[*] When I got back to Washington, he had just straightened my thinking out to such a point that it was a pleasure to be back in the driver's seat again."

The next year Eisenhower was a candidate for President.[†] We went to play Cornell. This time I was the senior naval officer present, and I sat next to Deane Malott, president of Cornell University. It was another privilege and pleasure. But Deane Malott turned to me at luncheon, he said, "Captain, did you ever know Swede Hazlett?"

"Sir, I knew him, but not well."

"Oh, he was one of the most genteel, lovely people I ever knew," said Deane Malott. "But as a thinker, I don't know anybody who was able to think a problem through as clearly as Swede Hazlett. He just had a magnificent mind."

Well, I was still secretary of the academic board, and my World War II squadron commander, Duke Chandler, had retired from the Navy and become president of William & Mary.[‡] He asked the President of the United States to make the address at his inauguration at William & Mary in Williamsburg.

I asked the Navy to let me be the representative in the academic procession of the Naval Academy. Harvard was well represented as the oldest university, and St. John's was there as the second, and William & Mary now the third, and they were getting a new president. So it was quite an occasion, and there were more caps and gowns around. One thing that stood out was the white uniform from the Naval Academy.

---

[*] Eisenhower, who held the rank of general of the Army, served as Chief of Staff from 19 November 1945 to 7 February 1948.
[†] In 1952 Eisenhower ran for President of the United States as a Republican and won the election against Democrat Adlai Stevenson.
[‡] Alvin Duke Chandler retired from the Navy as a vice admiral in November 1951.

At any rate, I went to luncheon at the president's house, and I saw President Eisenhower again. He was sailing with his brothers on the Williamsburg for Annapolis to join Admiral Joy for luncheon and for chapel on Sunday morning.* Admiral Joy went down with Mrs. Joy and Mrs. Buchanan and Mrs. Keith, and Captain Buchanan, the commandant of midshipmen, and his senior aide Keith.† We sat on the fantail while the ladies were down with Mamie getting ready to go to chapel.‡ We had a chance to chat before the time. Admiral Joy asked a question which I remember, and I want to recall that, because it's interesting as to what purposes the President has now. He said, "Mr. President, did you enjoy your trip on the Williamsburg?"

The President said, "Admiral, I enjoyed it so much that I regret that I listened to my brother Milton," whom he pointed to, sitting nearby, "who told me that the American people would not stand for having this magnificent ship at my beck and call, with nothing other than to be a yacht for the President of the United States, that they would think that was extravagant, and they wouldn't stand for it. I had to agree with him that I thought it was more than the job required to have a ship of this size at my disposal. I am turning it back to the Navy, primarily at their suggestion. I wish I weren't, because I enjoyed this trip." And it was his only trip on it.

Captain Buchanan had a chance to say something to the President, and I don't remember what he said. I remember what I said, and it was this: "Mr. President, let me ask you why, sir, when I sat next to the president of the great university of Columbia, the President asked me if I knew Swede Hazlett and then heaped encomiums on his head, and how it happened that the president of another great university, a year later, Cornell, I sat next to Deane Malott, and he said, 'Do you know Swede Hazlett? He has the most magnificent mind I've ever seen.' Could you tell me, sir, how this came about?"

The President of the United States didn't pay any attention to me. He turned and looked. "Milton, Milton, you remember Swede Hazlett, don't you?"

---

* Vice Admiral C. Turner Joy, USN, was superintendent of the Naval Academy from August 1952 to August 1954.
† Captain/Rear Admiral Charles A. Buchanan, USN, served from 1952 to 1954 as the Naval Academy's commandant of midshipmen.
‡ Mamie was President Eisenhower's wife.

Milton said nothing to the President of the United States. He turned and looked at me and said, "Captain, that was the greatest mutual admiration society that ever existed in the world. They all grew up together in Abilene, Kansas, and went to high school together."

Well, I think David Eisenhower would enjoy that.

Q: You told me earlier that you also had some association with David Eisenhower's father.

Admiral Keith: He was an exchange duty officer. He was in the same position under me that I was when I first went to the Naval Academy. He was an exchange officer, a thing that we arranged for a West Point officer to come to us, and we'd send a naval officer up there. I think we still do that, and send them to the Air Force Academy too.

Q: What are your memories of John Eisenhower? What was he like as an officer to work with?

Admiral Keith: He did his job. He was liked by the midshipmen.

There isn't really much chance, unless by some reason, out of 24 or 36 company officers--36 companies now, they had 24, I think, in my day--that you give them some particular job to do that the commandant wants accomplished, and therefore, they come and make a report to you. But the company officers report to the executive officer, and they report through a battalion officer. The battalion officer is usually a commander, and then there's a captain, the head of six battalion officers. There isn't an intimate association like it is with eight officers on a destroyer, ten officers on a destroyer. So I had him in my house for--if I had anything to say about the Army, I think that the Army junior officers are a whole lot more reticent in the presence of rank.

*   *   *

You remember I told you about taking promotion examinations in Washington when I was a junior lieutenant? When I got to the Naval Academy as secretary of the academic board, this business of testing examinations came back to my mind. The reason it came back is because we were closely associated with the Educational Testing Service at Princeton, New Jersey, in preparing the Naval Academy's substantiating examinations for high school students' certificates of graduation. We gave them certain substantiating examinations in science, English, and history. I made a couple of trips to Princeton, talking to them, learning what they were doing.

In doing this, I said to them one day, "Would you be interested in testing some of the questions that you propound as part of your testing service?" I said, "We get in a number of candidates every year, and they're assembled in a class at the Naval Academy for two or three months. We could give you a couple of days to try out on people from all the 48 states, various high schools and schools, questions that you want to test, to see whether they're fair to go into your testing service examinations."

They jumped at the chance. I'm sure they don't do it now, because there are no substantiating examinations for the Naval Academy. The Naval Academy uses the regular SAT scores.[*] So I don't think that's any longer done, but it's an interesting sidelight into the educational process at the Naval Academy.

In my day, of course, every midshipman took the same course. But we were very interested in whether or not what we were doing was equal to the standards of the other colleges and universities. For instance, when I went to Cornell, as I was talking about a few minutes ago, I went up the day before the game. Then I spent all of Saturday morning with the physics department at Cornell, trying to see whether or not our physics requirements at the Naval Academy were comparable to theirs. Fortunately, I ran into a man who had been on the Naval Academy Postgraduate School faculty; he was the head of the physics department at Cornell by the time I got there. He was very interested in helping. What it worked out to be was that we found out that the physics that was required of a graduate chemist was exactly the same physics that were requiring, and we weren't graduating physicists; that the chemistry that was required of a physics majors was exactly the same as the chemistry that they required of a physics major, so that we got a comparable understanding.

---

[*] SAT--Scholastic Aptitude Test.

We did the same sort of thing by contact with MIT. Penn State was another testing ground for us. Admiral Boone and I spent the morning of a Penn State football game in their applied physics laboratory.* They had a contract with the Navy for developing reversible-pitch propellers of all sizes. The reversible-pitch propellers that are now driving our turbine ships were a development from Penn State--not that we had anything to do with it. But knowing what's going on and having an opportunity to go in and see the development of work, as part of an entirely different project, going to a football game, is, to me, part of the interest that your career generates in the individual. Admiral Boone and I were fascinated, just seeing what they were doing and what they could do in that field.

Q: How much did you get involved with the process of accreditation of the Naval Academy's curriculum?

Admiral Keith: I think that was all done before I ever got involved in it. I think they had a program to look at our library at one time while I was there, but I didn't get involved in it particularly.

At Cornell I did see them in the physics department using television. This was '52. They were using television for physics laboratory work, in demonstrations by professors, particularly. I was able to get, when I got back, 18 television sets. Whether it was surplus or where they came from, I don't remember now, but I did get them. I turned them over to our department of physics and chemistry, electrical engineering, and in hindsight I think that I did the wrong thing.

I turned it over to the senior physics professor, Colonel Thomson.† I should have called in everybody in the department and said, "Now, here is a new way to present your

---

* Rear Admiral Walter F. Boone, USN, was superintendent of the Naval Academy from August 1954 to March 1956.
† Professor Earl W. Thomson taught at the Naval Academy, 1919-42 and 1945-59. He was widely known as "Slipstick Willie" because of his prowess with a slide rule. He held a reserve commission as a colonel, and from July 1942 to October 1949 he was on active duty in the Army's coast artillery. For more on Thomson see Shipmate magazine, published by the Naval Academy Alumni Association, June 1982, page 13.

experiments that you want to show people. This is a new gadget. We want all sorts of ideas as to how to do it." The midshipmen were not impressed with the utilization made of it by Colonel Thomson. I'm very fond of Colonel Thomson. I thought he was a wonderful professor. I went to him when I was a midshipman, and I knew him when he had finished his war years, in which he did very well on a staff. But I think a broader utilization of those things, and experimentation as to how they should be used, would have had much more lasting results. I'm sure they use them all sorts of ways now. But that many years ago, they didn't impress the midshipmen, anyhow. I thought that so many experiments were done by professors to demonstrate a theory or demonstrate this, that, or the other, and you were always trying to peer around the guy's head in front of you, to see what the professor was doing.

Q: What was the shortcoming in the way he used them?

Admiral Keith: No way I can tell you. I just don't know. I'm telling you what the midshipmen told me. I didn't go and see it done; I didn't have time.

*   *   *

On the subject of aptitude, in my day we had a great deal of congressional interest in the people that they sent to the Naval Academy. But the aptitude system is to eliminate as well as to pick out the good. If you find someone who does not measure up to the standards that you think he should, you can recommend him for a lack of aptitude discharge.

When I was secretary of the academic board, we had a young man who was marked down when he first got an aptitude grade as a sophomore or a youngster. Everybody that marked him said he had a great potential, but that he was not using it, or, if he was using it, it was to lead people into trouble and not to lead them the way a leader should for good. In his second-class year they said the same thing about him--"great potential but misuses it, won't use it, won't do the things that he should do to demonstrate what his competences are." Finally, when he was at the end of his first term as a first classman, we recommended discharge.

A congressman from Arizona, I believe he was, got pretty irate about this. He said, "I don't think your aptitude system is any good. It kicked out a man of mine from West Point not long ago. I don't think you people know what you're doing." So he told the Secretary of the Navy that he would fight it in Congress, if necessary, to keep this man from going. These letters were going back and forth. I got into a car and drove up to his office one afternoon. Went in and asked to see him, and he said he'd see me. I told him why I'd come and that I wanted to talk to him about his midshipman and about the aptitude system. I told him what I've told you--that we made it as broad-gauged as we could, that we had determined that this young man was not a good candidate and that we shouldn't send him into the fleet to lead men and be in charge of men.

He said, "Well, West Point is a beautiful example of what an aptitude system does. They discharged one of my appointees, and he went into the Air Force. When he went through aviation training, he was rated the top man in his class, in every way superior."

I said, "Yes, sir. We said about this midshipman we're talking about, and probably West Point said the same thing about him--that he had great potential, but he wouldn't use it. That he was throwing away all the good things that God had put in him that he wasn't using them. We weren't going to give him a chance to go out and misuse his talent to the detriment of the enlisted men that he bossed. When he finally got kicked out of West Point, it woke him up. And when he went into the Air Force, he went with the idea that he had better buckle down and show what he could do." I said, "West Point did, and we want to do to this midshipman just what he needed and what his father or somebody should have done a long time ago, and that's kick him right square in the ass."

He looked at me, and I said, "When he got that boot at West Point, he woke up, and what he did in the Air Force is proof that every one of those fitness reports recognized that he should be at the top, but he wouldn't do it. Now, what do you want us to do--to say, 'Oh, he'll be fine when he gets out in the fleet.'? I don't think we should be asked to do that, sir. If he goes in the Air Force or goes anywhere and succeeds, it's because he got the kick that he needed to wake him up." He withdrew his objection.

*   *   *

I took command of the Missouri in April of 1954, with the understanding that she was going to go out of commission within six months of the time that I took command.*

Q: Had that been publicly announced yet?

Admiral Keith: If it hadn't, it was known to me as the force commander's chief of staff.† Whether it was announced before I took command or subsequently, my memory doesn't tell me. But it was pretty well known that she was going out of commission.

The Missouri had just finished an overhaul in Norfolk shipyard.‡ She was at anchor when I arrived in Norfolk from Newport, in Hampton Roads. I took command, and we sailed the next day for refresher training at Guantanamo.

Q: Could you describe the experience of getting her under way from anchorage the first time?

Admiral Keith: It was a very difficult proceeding. Hampton Roads, as you know, is a very sizable anchorage, and the Missouri was the only ship in it. There were no merchantmen anywhere nearby, and she was headed up the James River, so it was obvious that a twist was necessary to head for sea. I decided to twist starboard ahead one-third and port back one-third. The ship began to swing very quietly and nicely to port. Then I went from one-third ahead to full ahead, one-third back to full back, and very shortly the Missouri went into irons. My exec was on the bridge with me, and he had great experience in the

---

* Keith commanded the USS Missouri (BB-63) from 1 April 1954 to 18 September 1954.
† Prior to this Keith had served as chief of staff to Commander Destroyer Force Atlantic Fleet.
‡ The USS Missouri (BB-63) was commissioned 11 June 1944. She had a standard displacement of 45,000 tons and full-load displacement of 57,600 tons. She was 887 feet long and 108 feet in the beam. Her top speed was 33 knots. In the mid-1950s she was armed with nine 16-inch guns and 20 5-inch guns, and 18 40-mm quad mounts. She remained in active service until decommissioned on 26 February 1955.

Missouri, having been with her in Korea and through her overhaul.* He was a good ship handler, and he said, "Captain, why did you do that?"

I said, "I read a book, and the book I read, Bob, was by Admiral Cunningham of the British Navy, who said, 'Those of you who go from command of a destroyer to command of a modern behemoth, you'll be astounded at the magnificent reluctance of the latter to answer helm and engine orders.'† He proceeded, then, in his book, to tell us that he went from command of a destroyer to the Rodney. And his first orders were to proceed to sea, leading the fleet to sea out of Plymouth. I had the same experience he did in terms of slow response in shallow water, which is why I put on more power. I never, in my tour on Missouri, had any time to call upon full power, in any sense of an emergency, until we were at San Francisco on our way to our last resting place in Bremerton.‡

*　　*　　*

Missouri was a ship that would answer her helm and engine orders at the appropriate time, if you were lucky, and if you had some background in what you were trying to do. There are several sensations that you sort of think back on in your naval career. Until I got the Missouri, one of the biggest highlights came when I was gunnery officer on a 1,500-ton destroyer. I remembered riding that director when we were on what was known as the Aylwin line, developed by Deak Parsons when he was executive officer.§ This was a tactic for night search, where you put a whole squadron out at an interval equal

---

* The executive officer was Commander James R. "Bob" North, USN.
† Keith was probably remembering a recently published book by Admiral of the Fleet Andrew B. Cunningham. It was A Sailor's Odyssey (New York: E. P. Dutton, 1951). On page 140 Cunningham discussed his experience in taking command of the battleship Rodney: "To one who had never commanded anything larger than a small cruiser the Rodney appeared enormous. This, and her odd bridge arrangements, gave me some qualms at first about handling her in narrow waters. But beyond the remoteness of the stem and a majestic dilatoriness in answering her helm and propellers, I eventually found her little different from the smaller ships to which I had been accustomed."
‡ In September 1954 the Missouri began the inactivation process at the Puget Sound Naval Shipyard, Bremerton, Washington.
§ Lieutenant Commander William Sterling Parsons, USN, was executive officer of the Aylwin in the late 1930s. In August 1945, as a captain, he became much better known because of his role as weaponeer for the mission in which a B-29 dropped an atomic bomb on Hiroshima, Japan.

to twice the night visibility, and you went in on a search line, until such time as one of the squadrons made contact with the assault force, on which you were going to launch a torpedo attack. Then you joined up at 25 knots and went boiling in to make your attack. You had no radar, you couldn't see, but you were sitting high up in the air with the wind rushing by. It was a wonderful sensation, until you grew up and found out just how much there was out there for you to see, when we developed and installed radar. So that was a wonderful sensation. You said to yourself, "Boy, were we lucky!"

Now, comparable to that rush of wind in your face is to be on the upper level, 11 decks up on the Missouri, which is your handling station when you're maneuvering, because that's the only place you could see bow and stern.* To come through a formation that's going 15 to 20 knots in one direction, and you're rejoining from ahead, and you go through the formation, either in daylight or in darkness, to take your position at 25 knots, that is a ship-handling sensation that even beats the one of riding the destroyers.

Q: When did you discover that the Missouri had greater backing power than her sisters?

Admiral Keith: I'm one who sort of takes a good look before I go somewhere, to see whether or not there's any information I might gather about my new command. I found out that the boiler room for one of the Kentucky class had been installed at the destroyer engineering school.† The boilers on the destroyers and the boilers on the battleship were practically the same in that era, so these boilers were used for instruction. So when I was coming from the Destroyer Force Atlantic to command of Missouri, I had gone down to take a little engineering review at the destroyer engineering school in Newport.‡

I found out a few things that were there, such as backing power was limited by the fact that you had to secure your high-pressure steam, superheated steam, before you went

---

* The 08-level primary conning station in the Missouri was 11 decks above the waterline.
† Construction of the Iowa-cass battleship Kentucky (BB-66) was suspended 17 February 1947 when she was 72.1% complete. Her turbines were used in the construction of the replenishment ships Sacramento (AOE-1) and Camden (AOE-2) when they were built in the 1960s.
‡ The flagship for Destroyer Force Atlantic Fleet was based in Newport.

into port. When I got to the Missouri, I found out that some genius in the past had rigged a set of mirrors so that the flow meter for the super-heated steam was visible to the water tenders in the boiler room.* That meant they could control the superheat as well there when you were going into port as they could at any other time. Otherwise, if you couldn't see the flow meter, you couldn't use superheated steam. That's a rough explanation of the engineering reason. This gave me double the backing power in the Missouri that the other ships had. So that backing down for anchoring was more in line with what I was used to in destroyers.

Q: You told me a charming story, before we turned the tape recorder on, about when you encountered Whitey Taylor, and he found out about your backing capability in the Missouri.

Admiral Keith: Well, Whitey was the base commander at Guantanamo, and the Wisconsin went in with the usual battleship approach--a few knots here, and a stop and drift, and a few knots, and a few turns and stop and drift.† Then I came in and was able to back down with my superior backing power, and Whitey wanted to know just what was the difference between the Missouri and Wisconsin. I said, "Whitey, you know that the only difference is in the commanding officer's abilities." [Laughter] Finally, I told him what the difference was, but he was an old friend that I could make such a statement to.

* * *

The Missouri gave you lots of opportunities to put into practice things that you had sort of picked up along the way. I never enjoyed making personnel inspections, with everybody lined up in a row, in order to find out whether their hair was cut. I always felt that was the job of the petty officer, and it wasn't the job of the captain to go around. If people were doing their jobs, it was unnecessary for me to have to worry about it. So on the Missouri, I had the chance to put some theories into practice.

---

* Water tender was a rating that Admiral Keith remembered from his World War II service. In 1948 the name of the rating was changed to boilerman, which it remained until 1956.
† Rear Admiral Edmund B. Taylor, USN.

I conducted my first captain's inspection one Saturday morning on the Missouri, and I had my yeoman make notes of faults found. I was looking for a division that had no faults. I found two, and I publicly called to the exec and told him to get the liberty cards for the men in those divisions and send them on liberty immediately. I said that I would not inspect their living compartments that day, because I felt certain that if they were perfect at formation, there was no need for me to look at their living quarters.

The next week, I had a great deal of trouble finding fault with any division, because the petty officers had taken charge, and I was a little hesitant as it how it was going to be down below, but it looked all right. The divisions turned out at quarters beautifully.

The background for that is that I was required, as a division officer in the Arizona, many, many years before, as an ensign or jaygee, to face my division inboard, have them about-face, and then the inspecting admiral inspected fore and aft. He had them take their hats off; he had them hold their trouser legs up to see if they had garters on. He looked at their shoes. Then he took their jumpers off and inspected all the way. When he got to the last man of 75 men I had paraded at quarters, the little sleeve on his undershirt was ripped from the main body of the undershirt. And he turned to me and he said, "Young man, that man has ruined your whole division." I thought that was unnecessary, but that's the only fault he found. Ergo, when I got to the Missouri, I had a chance on a battleship to do something different.

As a captain and on the Missouri I had a good chance to do this, because there were many times on our cruise to Europe that summer when we'd have a need to overhaul a feed pump, overhaul a pump that was necessary to have the speed available that we wanted the next day. At 8:00 o'clock reports at night I would be told that I had a crew that was going to be working all night, and they expected to have it ready in the morning.

I felt certain that if I left a call with the quartermaster to come and call me at 2:30 in the morning that it would be all over the ship. The chief master-at-arms would be there, ready to escort me down Broadway, to whatever fireroom I was heading for, to see how this pump work was getting on.* So I had an alarm clock, which I set for 2:30. Then I

---

* "Broadway" is the nickname of a long fore-to-aft passageway on the third deck of an Iowa-class battleship.

would get up, dress, and make my own way where I wanted to go. I got down and had a cup of coffee with the men that were working on that pump. I felt it was important for them to know that I knew that they were giving me that kind of assistance to do the job I was required to do.

Q: So you wanted to give that to the men on the job without acting like you were showing off.

Admiral Keith: Well, I wanted them to know that I knew it, but I didn't want to--well, if you want to call it showing off, but I didn't want to make a big thing of it.

One of the ports we visited on our midshipman cruise to Europe was Cherbourg. We were there to celebrate the tenth anniversary of the liberation of Cherbourg.[*] While we were in port, the Queen Elizabeth came in with Mr. Churchill, returning from a visit to the United States.[†] I came home from a dinner party given by the French naval community for the officers of the visiting American squadron, and I saw the Queen Elizabeth. I was able to get hold of a yeoman, and I got him to give me a rough draft of a letter that I dictated, which we finalized and sent down to the Queen Elizabeth. I'd like to tell you what that was:

"The Honorable Sir Winston Churchill, SS Queen Elizabeth. Sir: On the occasion of your stop at Cherbourg, it is my privilege to send you the most respectful greetings of the officers, midshipmen, and men of the United States Ship Missouri, flagship of the 1954 midshipman training squadron. As this historic ship nears its September inactivation date, it is our great privilege to assist in the education of our prospective naval officers in the greatest of all schools--experience at sea. Our purpose and our hope is that they may contribute their share in the future to the everlasting aim of all men of good will--peace in our world. Your example of unstinting and unselfish service is an inspiration to each of us. Very respectfully and most sincerely, Taylor Keith, United States Navy, Commanding."

---

[*] Cherbourg was liberated by Allied soldiers in June 1944, a few weeks after the amphibious assault on Normandy on D-Day.
[†] Queen Elizabeth was a large Cunard Lines passenger ship that made regular transatlantic runs.

"Ten Downing Street, Whitehall, July 6, 1954. My dear Captain Keith: I am much obliged to you for your letter and wish to thank the officers and midshipmen and men of the United States Ship Missouri for their kind message of greetings on my arrival at Cherbourg this morning. I am touched that you should have taken this action on their behalf, and send you all my very best wishes. Yours sincerely, Winston S. Churchill."

Q: What was the date on your letter to him?

Admiral Keith: It was the same date, the sixth of July. But all I did was make a copy of this and put it in my scrapbook. I would like to have it on a sheet of Missouri stationery, with the commission pennant on it, but I never did it. But I thought if I could put it on this record, that that would get it into history anyhow. But I thought it was nice of him to write to me, and I enjoyed writing to him.

We visited Lisbon as part of our port visits on this cruise to Europe, and we were to anchor in Lisbon in waters that were reached by going through a shoal where the Missouri drew more water than was available, except at the very high tide. They sent two pilots on board to take the Missouri into this restricted port. We knew, in general, where we were going, but not specifically where our anchorage was to be. So as we approached this very narrow and shallow spot, a sailing vessel, a lugger, came bearing down on me on my starboard hand, having the right of way to starboard and the right of way because she was a sailing vessel.

Each pilot, in turn, would turn from his position at the windows on the bridge of the Missouri and wave his hands, that she was going to fall off and let us go by. But she held on. The pilots continued to insist, so I had to take command of the ship away from a pilots. The lugger sailed ahead of me into the clear waters, and we were able to proceed, unrammed by the lugger.

My flag officer was Ruthven Libby, and with the jingle of bells that showed we were going ahead again, Libs appeared at the top of the ladder from the flag bridge, just below the Missouri bridge.* He had only one comment before he returned to his area and said, "Taylor, I thought you'd won yourself a lugger." [Laughter]

So we reached our anchorage, and, you know, that same lugger came out that afternoon and rammed our stern while we were at anchor. Now, this time we were safe. We reported it all to the American Embassy, and I don't know whether they ever did anything about it or not. But that was one of the experiences and pleasantries of the duty in the Missouri.

There were three or four trained officers of the deck on the Missouri when I went through shakedown training. Then every one of them was detached from the ship before we started on this midshipman training cruise. So we moved up the junior officers to take us through refresher training. Then, before I went to the West Coast in September, I had another set, because the Bureau of Naval Personnel took all the officers off who wanted to stay in the Atlantic and not go west, and put on people who wanted to go to the West Coast. So I had to find three more officers to stand watch for me.

There are so many things about watch-standing that are significant, but the main thing is that I felt you should recognize your time in command first as an opportunity to learn yourself--the abilities and your ability to handle a ship--and then that you should afford to your other officers an opportunity to learn and gain from their experience in serving in your ship.

Every head of department on the Missouri during my six-month tenure had enough opportunities on that cruise to Europe to handle the ship alongside fueling, so that I could say that each of them was qualified to do it. The ship handled so nicely and steadily that I had three midshipmen standing watch on the bridge when we were fueling in the nice, quiet waters off Bermuda. They were all of the class of 1955 at the Naval Academy, and all three of them actually took command of the Missouri for a period alongside, wherein they changed the ship's heading, and they changed the turns to the engines on their own. I don't remember what those three names were. I've always meant to write to the class of '55 and

---

* Rear Admiral Ruthven E. Libby, USN, was Commander Battleship Cruiser Force Atlantic Fleet and served as commander of the midshipman training squadron for this cruise in 1954. The oral history of Libby, who retired as a vice admiral, is in the Naval Institute collection.

ask them to put a request in their class notes--to ask those three people to write to me to see if they remember that privilege, which I thought it was, handling the Missouri while fueling.

Q: I've seen a picture in which the Missouri and New Jersey steamed alongside for a time together, for a transfer, and the New Jersey band serenaded with "The Missouri Waltz."

Admiral Keith: [Laughter] During the cruise that summer, the only surgeon with us was in the New Jersey. The night before we were to put the football team from the Naval Academy ashore in Bermuda to go on early leave, before we went to Guantanamo for short-range battle practice, our doctor came up and said he had an emergency appendectomy that couldn't wait.[*] I was on the bridge, and Admiral Libby was below me. I ran down the ladder and said, "I've got to go alongside the New Jersey to put a patient on board. Will you authorize, and will you tell him I'm on my way?"

Then I moved the Missouri from her position in the center of the formation to alongside the New Jersey, at 25 knots, with all the midshipmen on deck to watch a smoker, just at dusk. I went alongside, and our lines went over. I was in position on one bell, and I cleared from alongside at full speed and was back in my position inside of a half an hour. I felt that this was a fairly good piece of luck for me to have this opportunity to let midshipmen see their prospective commandant of midshipmen, which I was to be within two months, handle a ship. And it was quite a thrill to move that ship alongside her sister ship in an expeditious manner.

Q: I've seen the picture of that in the New Jersey ship's paper, and that was the occasion. I remember that there was a smoker going on at the time.

Admiral Keith: That was the night.

---

[*] This incident was the night of 17 July 1954.

Q: That's usually an occasion for the midshipmen to get a bit of revenge at the officers that had been training them. Did you have a smoker like that in the Missouri also?

Admiral Keith: No. I don't think that this is part of history, but, as I've told you, there was a poem written in the last edition of the Missouri paper by a midshipman. It was wonderfully conceived and carried out as a poem of about 16 to 20 stanzas. It covered practically every division on the ship, and the characters in each division were named. They even talked about the kindly chief master-at-arms who woke them up so gently every morning. It was just full of humor, full of fun. To me they said, "To Captain Keith, our thanks abound. Your ship is really cool. Now, how about more weekends when you take over at our school?" Now they have so many weekends they don't know what to do with them all at the Naval Academy, but they were quite a privilege in my day.

Q: Was there a round of social activities laid on in Lisbon and Cherbourg for the midshipmen?

Admiral Keith: Oh, yes. The minister to Lisbon became one of my friends. He's from Phoenix, Mr. Minotto.[*] He died a few years ago. He was a great friend of Admiral Libby's, a great friend of mine. His wife comes to Coronado every summer. We still see her and exchange dinner parties and things when she comes.

In France Admiral Libby went off to Paris for a little vacation, and he left me to do the honor of making a presentation to the maritime museum, the Musee de Marine in Cherbourg. They took over the old Fort Du Roule in Cherbourg and made it into a museum of World War II. It was really a magnificent display of all types of equipment that we used in the landing. The thing that I had never known--here it was 1954--I did not know that we had laid a fuel pipeline, under the English Channel, and that most of the fuel that was used by Patton and the tank corps of World War II came through that pipeline.

---

[*] James Minotto, chief of mission to Portugal for the Mutual Security Agency.

Q: Its nickname was PLUTO, which stood for pipeline under the ocean.

Admiral Keith: [Laughter] Well, I'm sure that's it. But in 1954 I was not aware of it. I'm aware of it now.

Q: What do you remember about Admiral Libby as the squadron commander during that cruise?

Admiral Keith: Well, the first thing about Admiral Libby is a feeling of amazement. He took 21 ships into the English Channel at night, in a circular formation, he having the conn. I stood in flag plot and watched him while Bob North was on the bridge. Admiral Libby realized that he couldn't maneuver these ships in circular formation, so he put them in a column. But there was a considerable amount of traffic. He took 21 ships through the English Channel without ever having to say to any ship in that column, "You're on your own to maneuver to clear the blip that I have on your starboard hand." He anticipated to such an extent that he would see a blip appear on his radar screen far enough away that a slight deviation of his course would give that ship enough clearance. He judged their speed vis-a-vis ours to the point that I was absolutely amazed. I don't know a man whose brain I admire any more.

He was one of the Navy's brilliant thinkers.[*] But he was also a man who could apply his knowledge to tactical maneuvering. I had been an employer of tactical graphics when you used a pair of parallel rulers to maneuver yourself around--or if you were lucky, you had one of the protractors that were anchored to your chartboard and you could use that. But it was long before we had any of the modern abilities to maneuver or to gauge maneuvering. But to see what he could do with from the PPI scope was a matter of amazement to me.[†]

---

[*] Libby stood third among the 539 graduates in the Naval Academy class of 1922.
[†] PPI--plan position indicator, a type of radar that presents essentially a geographical picture with one's own ship in the center of the scope and surrounding ships, planes, and land areas shown in their respective positions in terms of range and bearing.

He had Arleigh Burke as a cruiser division commander with him that summer.* He had Oley Sharp as the skipper of the cruiser that Burke rode, and they worked as a team extremely well.† They had a rapport with each other. I sent the obituary editorial from the local paper to Arleigh Burke when Admiral Libby died.‡ He had a very beautiful tribute written by the local editor of the paper.

Q: Of course, he'd been involved with that paper, so there was a closer tie than for most.

Admiral Keith: They knew something about him, yes. But this man who was the editor then came long after Libby did. I wrote to the editor and told him I had appreciated what he had written about Libby, and I sent it to Arleigh, and he enjoyed it. Arleigh now has bad eyes, and he wrote me a very nice letter back saying that he was having to rely on his "seeing-eye wife" to be his scrivener.

Q: Maybe you could say a bit more about Commander North, your executive officer. Certainly he had a good deal of experience with the ship, having been with her off Korea.

Admiral Keith: He had been selected for captain, but BuPers would not make him a captain--even though he had made his number--until he was in a captain's billet. He was still in a commander's billet as executive officer.

I found out that there were two of his classmates, junior to him, who were going to be division commanders of destroyers on that cruise that summer to Europe. They were both in captain's billets; therefore they were made captains. I got on the hot wire to Washington and said that I could see no problem in having North as a captain, that if there was any question of who was commanding the Missouri, then they needed a new

---

* Rear Admiral Arleigh A. Burke, USN, Commander Cruiser Division Six. The following year Burke became Chief of Naval Operations.
† Captain U. S. Grant Sharp, USN, commanded the heavy cruiser Macon (CA-132) in 1953-54. He later became a four-star admiral.
‡ Vice Admiral Libby died 28 July 1986. He had been an executive with Coply newspapers following his retirement from the Navy in 1960.

commanding officer. I told them that they should get busy and make North a captain, and so he was a captain for all the social activities and protocol on the visit to Europe.

He was a doer. He came home one night in Cherbourg, and they were leading some sailor of the Missouri up the gangway, and he was bloody and had been hit with a broken bottle, apparently. North went to work, and he went to the other ships on the pier, and he caught the two men off another ship that had hit him with the bottle. So he didn't wait for instructions. He saw a job to be done, and he did it. But anybody who has gotten to flag rank in the Navy has been blessed with able assistance along the way, and Bob was just one.

I want to make an overall comment about the conduct of the men ashore. When Libby took the cruise to Europe, he had a remarkable record over there. He had very little in the way of trouble, that night at Cherbourg being an exception.

Q: One of the very interesting events of that spring of '54, on that midshipman cruise, was that all four ships of the class steamed together on one occasion.[*] What do you remember of that?

Admiral Keith: We tried hard, but we never did get all four of them in line. We got four of them in one picture. But they were ordered out there by Admiral Libby for the purpose of getting a picture with all four of them together. That was the first time they'd ever been together.

Q: It was the last also.

Admiral Keith: No, they were all in the Caribbean when I went through in Missouri on my way to Bremerton to put her out of commission.[†] I came out of a rainstorm, and they were all there. Admiral Cooper, who had the batdiv at that time, flew over and had lunch with

---

[*] This was on 7 June 1954, as the Missouri and New Jersey were beginning their midshipman cruise to Europe.
[†] Actually, the New Jersey (BB-62) was in overhaul at the Norfolk Naval Shipyard as the Missouri made her voyage to Bremerton.

me, then helicoptered back to their ship, and I went on my way.* That was his farewell to me.

In Norfolk Admiral Jerauld Wright called up one morning and said he was going to come down to pay a last visit to the Missouri, but that he didn't want any honors, no folderol.† He came down, and I had the crew paraded at quarters. He said, "I thought I told you I wanted no honors, no inspection. I just wanted to come down and pay my respects to the Missouri."

I said, "Admiral, I feel, sir, that when the commander in chief comes aboard my ship, that my crew is entitled to pay their respects to him, too, sir. And they paraded in your honor, and I hope you'll have a word to say to them."

He took the mike and made a very gracious talk. But you never get into trouble with your superiors by always doing what they want. He really didn't want to make any fuss about that, but I'm sure he appreciated my feelings in the matter, and he was glad to talk to the men.

Q: You mentioned before we started taping that you'd had deck tennis games during the course of the cruise. How was that worked out?

Admiral Keith: Well, they just trained turret one and turret two to port and put a net in between them, right down on the port side, and we played there. That gives you a good deal of space when you get the turrets swung away there.

Q: Since the inactivation had already been announced, did you commence some of the preparations even before you got to Bremerton?

---

* Rear Admiral George R. Cooper, USN, Commander Battleship Division Two, visited the Missouri when she was near Cuba in late August.
† Admiral Jerauld Wright, USN, served as Supreme Allied Commander Atlantic and Commander in Chief Atlantic Fleet from April 1954 to March 1960.

Admiral Keith: Now, you want to talk about Bob North. The executive officer took over that as a job, and that's where he spent most of the summer: with the heads of departments, laying out his plans for the inactivation period. He had full instructions from whoever was in charge of inactivation, and there were plenty of precedents. We had laid up plenty of ships. It was under some particular command whose name I haven't the slightest recollection of. But Bob North took that on, and he put the ship out within the specified time. He put it out properly, and the proof of the pudding is in the fact that she went back in without any difficulty.

I went up to visit her when she was first brought down for her recommissioning at Long Beach.* I was on the New Jersey for luncheon. The captain of the New Jersey had me, he had my son, who was here on duty at the time, and his son, who was a midshipman, to lunch.†

Q: This is Captain Milligan.‡

Admiral Keith: That's right. He had us to lunch, and he also had the captain from the yard, who had the recommissioning of the Missouri as his project. The shipyard captain took us on a tour of the Missouri, what could be seen of it at the time. I have a picture taken of the three Keiths--R. T. S., all of them--on board the Missouri. He said that he was astounded that he didn't find a single double bottom with any water in it, that the ship was absolutely sound, and she was dry.

When the Missouri was recommissioned in San Francisco, the Secretary of Defense was there, as was the Secretary of the Navy.§ I had a chance to speak with the Secretary of

---

* In May 1984 the Missouri was towed from her mothball site at Bremerton, Washington, to be reactivated at the Long Beach Naval Shipyard.
† Captain R. T. S. Keith, Jr., USN; Midshipman R. T. S. Keith III, USN.
‡ Captain Richard D. Milligan, USN, commanded the USS New Jersey (BB-62) from 15 September 1983 to 7 September 1985.
§ Secretary of Defense Caspar Weinberger was the principal speaker when the Missouri was recommissioned at San Francisco on 10 May 1986.

Defense, and I said to him that I had been a previous skipper. He said, "I noted that. I saw your name in the list of the guests who were going to be here."

I said, "I feel pretty happy about the fact that they found her in such good condition, that she was dry and properly preserved."

The Secretary of Defense said, yes, and they found her electrical wiring in such good condition that he was able to make a statement in his speech at the commissioning that, "We do not have a 40-year-old ship; we have a five-year-old ship or eight-year-old ship" or whatever her age was, that she was that well laid up.

Now, that had nothing to do with R. T. S. Keith; that has only to do with the work of Bob North. But he was a very, very capable person.

Q: There was a rumor that she had some kind of a speed restriction as a result of the grounding at Hampton Roads in 1950. Is there any truth to that rumor?

Admiral Keith: Never that I heard of.

Q: So you weren't aware of any inhibitions that you had.

Admiral Keith: Nobody told me anything about it.

Q: What are your recollections of shooting the 16-inch guns while you were captain?

Admiral Keith: You could see a 16-inch bullet, and you couldn't see a 14-inch. At least I never have seen a 14-inch. But, of course, I fired 14-inch mostly from the turrets of the Arizona, and not where I was up on the deck to see them. But, as for concussion, I have a great deal more sensation of concussion from the 14-inch guns on the Texas than I do from the 16-inch guns on the Missouri, and this is the reason. We were firing a night battle practice in the Atlantic when I was an ensign, and I was a check-sight observer on a star-shell gun located on the upper deck, right aft of turret two on the Texas. We were there to see that the star-shell guns didn't get trained on the tugs that were towing the targets for the night battle practice.

However, the approach made by the tactical officer and division commander of the battleships that were to fire this practice, observed by my battleship division, didn't find the target early enough. When he did locate it, instead of getting all of the firing done while the target was forward of the beam, they ended up firing well trained aft. We were firing star shells out here from that gun, and the blasts from those things were right in my ear almost. I had, in the wind, put my chin strap down to my chin to keep my regulation cap on my head. When I got through, the grommets in my white cap cover had been pulled out by the concussion. So I say that the concussion from the 14-inch is worse than the concussion from the 16-inch, because they never fired the 16-inch gun that close to the captain of the Missouri's ears.

Q: You talked about the adjustments that come with ship handling, in going from a small ship to a capital ship. Were there any adjustments in the fact that you now have a separate mess and you don't have the opportunity to be as close to your officers as you did in the destroyer?

Admiral Keith: You sat at the table with your destroyer officers. You tried not to usurp the conversation, but to bring them all in through your talk. You are isolated as captain of a battleship. I had a beautiful mess in the Missouri.

You know that the battleships were given silver by the states. There was some dispute as to whether they were going to let the Missouri have anything other than the silver plates back, whether they could have the punchbowl, which was given to the first Missouri.[*] For one thing, we had to find out what the Navy did with the silver. The historical section of the bureau said we always return it to the states, so the Navy packed it up and sent the

---

[*] The earlier battleship Missouri (BB-11) was commissioned in 1903 and decommissioned in 1919.

Missouri silver back to Missouri. But when the Missouri became the surrender ship, this Missouri, the silversmiths of Missouri outdid themselves.[*]

They built 12 serving plates, about 10 to 12 inches in diameter, beautiful things. They built 12 silver goblets with the stems of them all in the shape of dolphins. And when you set a table with that and candlelit, it was a beautiful sight. Then I had most of the first class midshipmen on the cruise in to dinner with me during the summer, and they always came with some of my officers. So you could just see, as they came in and took a look, that they were impressed with what they were seeing. I was impressed with it. Don't get me wrong. I thought it was a pretty beautiful setting, and I loved to entertain there.

*   *   *

We went into San Francisco during our voyage to Bremerton. The pilot who came out to get me was an old friend, whose name today is gone from my memory. But he had been the pilot that I went in there on the Nitro, an ammunition ship, in 1934 and '35. I guess we made four or five visits to San Francisco within the year as we went up and down the coast. The pilot was, as I say, an old friend, but he hadn't handled a battleship since the war. He also, in the time since the war, was the pilot who, when one of hospital ships went aground on the Farallon Islands, went out and handled the tugs that got the ship off of the rocks.

So he was a man who had done well by the Navy, and he was going to be retired the next day, he told me as we were going into Hunters Point.[†] He missed his tide by about ten minutes, and we were to go into the pier at the big crane that we'd taken from Germany as reparations after World War II. We started in, and the outgoing tide caught the stern and started pushing it to starboard. He tried to correct it by pushing a little harder, and he finally went to full back and full ahead. I watched and watched, and gradually he got a little way on the ship, but his engine orders and his tugs hadn't corrected it. So I took command, backed emergency full, and stopped the ship. Then I returned it to the pilot because of the fact that he was going to retire the next day, and he put it alongside very nicely.

---

[*] The state presented a new silver service to the Missouri (BB-63) on 4 December 1948.
[†] Hunters Point Naval Shipyard, San Francisco.

When I left the ship, one of my friends who had been on the pier to meet me said, "I thought you had won yourself a pier. You were five feet from the pier when you stopped." [Laughter]

I had a very favorite young cousin and her husband who lived in San Francisco. While the Missouri was there, I asked them to come down and have lunch with me. Well, there was a great rivalry between Los Angeles and San Francisco as to who was going to have the most visitors during the time that we were there. They called up in San Francisco and said, "How many visitors did you have in Los Angeles?" Then they published it in the paper, "San Francisco is behind." So Sunday's visitors, we had to extend visiting hours in order to take care of all the people who wanted to go.

The curtains on my cabin were drawn so that I wouldn't have people looking in the windows as they wandered around the ship. The door opened, and in walked a man who said, "I'm from Missouri, and I know little old Harry. He's from my hometown, and I knew he would want me to see the whole ship, so I just came on in." [Laughter] So you run into all sorts of people and kinds.

Earlier we had been in Long Beach, where we got in late. When we arrived, I got a telephone call from one of the Navy's well-known characters, named Jack Bolton, from Baltimore, Maryland. He had gone up to Hollywood sometime in his life and gotten into the movie business. He called me and said, "Taylor, I've got a favor to ask of you. Jimmy Stewart and his two boys want to see the Missouri. Will you get them on board?"[*]

I said, "There's people who have been standing in line down here since 6:00 o'clock this morning. We just docked at 11:00 o'clock. We were two hours late, due to fog. How am I going to get the fellow?" Police officials had talked to me about plans for getting visitors on board and so forth and so on.

One of them said, "I know Jimmy Stewart. I'll go and pick him out of the line for you." So, sure enough, he goes out, and when he sees Jimmy Stewart come to the end of

---

[*] James Stewart was one of the most prominent movie actors of the period. For a picture of him and his two sons on the ship's surrender deck, see Paul Stillwell, Battleship Missouri: An Illustrated History (Annapolis: Naval Institute Press, 1996), page 233. The book contains many other pictures from Captain Keith's command tenure.

the line, he goes over and taps him on the shoulder, puts him in a police car, and brings him down and brings him on board.

I got a call from Bolton, and he said, "You're a miracle worker. Jimmy Stewart was just delighted with the way he was treated down there. He can't do enough for me now." [Laughter]

Q: You had a great attraction there.

Admiral Keith: The police do come in handy sometimes.

Q: Did you have any other contacts with official people in the state, other than the return of the silver?

Admiral Keith: No, not I. I'm sure that if you are around long enough, that you could do something like that. The New Jersey would have a particularly good chance, when she's in New York, to make the proper friendly gestures to the governor or some officials.

Somebody told me once that if I'd bring the Missouri up the little creek that runs by my home in Virginia, that the whole town of Warrenton would turn out to see it. But it doesn't fit, you know. And it doesn't get up the Mississippi River far enough for them to have a visit there.

Q: Well, speaking of tight fit, getting that ship through the Panama Canal is not all that easy. What are your recollections of that?

Admiral Keith: Somebody was asking me about the Missouri and the Panama Canal the other day. Oh, Admiral Putt Storrs's daughter was out here from South Carolina for

Christmas with him.* She came up and said that they were in Panama, and that they'd gone on board the Missouri.†

I said, "I was captain of the Missouri when she went through there."

She said, "Well, she certainly wasn't very pretty when we saw it."

I said, "What did you find?"

"Oh, there were black marks all over the side, and she was dirty-looking. She didn't look very well."

I said, "Well, she was dirty because she was 108 and a half feet wide, and the Panama Canal is 110 feet. We tried to save the sides as much as we could. We procured a lot of tires and hung them over the side to take up some of the shock as she bumped, as she was bound to do, going through there. She scraped on the side. Those black marks are all from that. But long before we got to Long Beach, she was much prettier." But it was a pretty tight fit. There again, crowds were standing on the dock in Panama. I tried to remember--the papers estimated how many people. I've got a lot of Missouri pictures upstairs in my memory book.

Q: Did you find that surrender deck plaque was a real attraction for visitors?

Admiral Keith: Before I took command of the Missouri, she went to New York after coming back from the Japanese surrender. They saw this big crowd around the plaque in New York, and they got down and somebody was trying to dig the plaque out. That's the reason they had the stanchions around it. Now there's a Marine guard on it whenever she's in port, or whenever visitors are on board.

Wherever we went with the Missouri, people had to stand in line before they could get on board. We had thousands of people. The decks were full. We couldn't let them go below decks, but they'd walk around topside. Even at that, you can't get 5,000, 6,000,

---

* Rear Admiral Aaron P. Storrs III, USN (Ret.) lived in Coronado, California, up to the time of his death in 1993.
† A few weeks before this interview, on 9 December 1986, the Missouri had gone through the Panama Canal near the conclusion of an around-the-world voyage.

10,000 people on board. I've forgotten what the numbers were. If you're interested, I can go up and get my book and look at it.

We went to Bremerton, and we had a great reception as we went into Seattle. They have Miss Puget Sound every year up there. Miss Puget Sound was there. They had Indian dances and put an Indian bonnet on me. I don't know whether it was in Bremerton or in Seattle, but the story's the same anyhow.

They had Miss Fish Fry--which is what I called Miss Seattle--hand me a brown paper bag, like this. Then the man holding the Indian chief's hat asked me, please, to unroll it. There was some writing on it that they wanted to get on the camera. As I started to unroll it, Miss Fish Fry reached over and gave me a kiss, and they took a picture. I had gotten this thing all unrolled, and it was full of mothballs in a paper bag. The caption on the picture that appeared in the paper was, "The battle-scarred old veteran stands petrified as the mothballs show a drop by the kiss of Miss Seattle." So you have things like that.

Then I was invited to a Rotary luncheon in Seattle. One of the people that I had known at the Naval Academy, who was one of our instructors, was Rusty Callow, who was the crew coach.[*] He was a perfectly splendid gentleman and a great influence for good on growing youth. I sat on the dais during the lunch, and I knew that the people on the dais were supposed to stand up and bow when they were introduced--and that's all. They asked the chaplain to ask a blessing before the dinner, and the chaplain's blessing was to the effect that this was the time of year that we were sending our children back to school and to colleges, and his prayer for the day was that the guidance and knowledge that we hope for would be made available to them, and that they would be able to absorb the guidance that was provided and the knowledge that was given.

So when I was introduced, I went down to the lectern, and I said, "I want to say something." They looked at me askance, naturally, because I wasn't supposed to do that. The Rotary prides itself on getting you in and out at the time they say they're going to. Well, they had a tremendous turnout, about 700 people. I said, "I ask pardon for my

---

[*] Russell S. Callow was on the Naval Academy faculty from 1950 to 1958.

presumption in taking this action, but I've had duty at the Naval Academy, where the preparation of youth for a career in the Navy is our responsibility, and I leave from here to go there and become the commandant of midshipmen, whose responsibility is for the integrity of the young officers we send out, to be sure that it is proper. I'm going back there, and I have previous knowledge of some of the people there. I want to tell you that there is one man who I feel has the greatest influence on growing youth of any instructor, teacher, or professor I've ever known, and his name is Rusty Callow, and he comes from Seattle Rotary to us at the Naval Academy." All 700 of them stood up. He had been coach, you know, of the crew at the University of Washington and was a revered person in Seattle. I wasn't in any trouble.

* * *

Then I went back to Annapolis. Sometimes you stir up a considerable amount of congressional interest and pressure on the Navy Department. One example was mentioned in the last history of the Naval Academy, which written here about four or five years ago.[*] Admiral Boone tells the story. He tells the basic parts of it. I'm going to tell you the story as it happened.

Admiral Boone has it in the story, and I don't know whether he names the secretaries involved or the assistant secretaries or not.[†] Anyhow, we had a sophomore or youngster--you recognize the term "youngster." I keep saying it. A Missouri graduate knows sophomore or second-year man.[‡] He doesn't know "youngster," but I'm sure you know the Naval Academy well enough for me to call them by what we called them.

A youngster saw a classmate cheat on a semi-annual examination, and he reported it. It was reviewed by his class honor committee, and they agreed with it. Then it went before the brigade honor committee, and they agreed that he was a cheater and didn't belong at the Naval Academy. Then it came to me, and I reviewed all the evidence, and I agreed. It went to the superintendent, and another review was made. Admiral Boone

---

[*] See Jack Sweetman, The U.S. Naval Academy: An Illustrated History (Annapolis: Naval Institute Press, 1979), page 211.
[†] As related in Sweetman's book, Albert Pratt, the Assistant Secretary of the Navy (Personnel and Reserve Forces), was the official involved.
[‡] The interviewer graduated from the University of Missouri.

forwarded it, recommending approval from Washington. Our boss then was the Chief of Naval Personnel. The Chief of Naval Personnel endorsed the superintendent's recommendation.

Then it went to the Secretary of the Navy. He was beginning to get a good deal of pressure from congressional sources to save this boy. How the political pressure developed, I don't know, but it was very strong in this particular case. He thought maybe there was one last hope, that he'd send it to the Chief of Naval Operations, and that he would disapprove it. But Arleigh Burke said, "I see nothing wrong with anything. I approve."

So then he called a meeting of his secretaries, and he dictated a letter telling the superintendent to take action short of discharge in this case. Well, that came to the ears of the commandant of midshipmen pretty soon from a sleuth in the Secretary's office. Who blew the cover, I don't know, and I ain't going to say, but I heard it, and I went to see the superintendent, and I went to see Captain Ed Miller, who was my executive officer.[*] We talked about it till 2:00 or 3:00 o'clock in the morning as to what we could do about it, but none of us had any solutions.

We were sending the teams off to West Point the next morning, and the superintendent and commandant always went over to see them off and wish them well. At the sendoff, I went up to Admiral Boone, and I said, "I want to see you in your office when this is over." So I went over and I said, "Finally, I have at least a chance to save the honor system at the Naval Academy. Would you call the Secretary of the Navy and ask him if he would see three midshipmen from the Naval Academy this afternoon on the subject of this case?"

He said, "What three midshipmen?"

I said, "Tell him he has a register in his office that lists every midshipmen, and he can pick any three of them he wants to talk to."

Now he said, "Suppose he tells me that he wants to have me name the midshipmen to talk to."

---

[*] Captain Edwin S. Miller, USN.

I said, "Well, we have a political system down here, too, and we have three men who've been elected by their classes, all of them at least 1,000 strong, as their class presidents. Ask him to talk to them. If he would see one more, we have a young man who's a classmate of this man who is the subject, and his name is [Unclear]. And he has just written a treatise on the honor system at the Naval Academy, and he supports it the way it stands. If they would see them and talk to them, and let them ask them questions about this case, they'd probably agree that the midshipman should go."

He said, "All right." He called the Secretary of the Navy, and the Secretary agreed. The superintendent took them in his car and drove them to Washington. He walked into the Secretary's office, where the other secretaries assembled with him. He introduced the midshipmen to the assembled crowd, turned around, and walked out. They said, "Don't leave, Admiral. We want to have you here too."

Admiral Boone, God bless him, said, "I'm sorry, sir. You have my recommendation. I want you to talk to these young men." Now, if you'll remember, the Naval Academy, the Chief of Naval Personnel, and the CNO all recommended that the discharge be approved. They talked to four midshipmen for four hours, and tore up their letter directing action short of discharge.[*]

Q: Honor prevailed.

Admiral Keith: Well, it would have destroyed the system. I don't know whether the system is still in effect; I think it is. I'm sure that this business of not reporting classmates when you see them violate their honor, that you don't want a dishonest man with you. If his shoes aren't shined, that's an entirely different proposition.

*   *   *

---

[*] In his account, Admiral Boone remembered one additional midshipman being present, the brigade commander.

When Admiral Smedberg became Superintendent of the Naval Academy, I was finishing up a tour as commandant of midshipmen there.* He had put the Iowa back in commission.† The midshipmen wanted to get some pictures of Admiral and Mrs. Smedberg to put in The Log, which is their weekly magazine. He was going over to have dinner the night before he took command, at the superintendent's house. He brought this newspaper-size scrapbook downstairs and said, "Now, just turn this over to the midshipmen and tell them they can use any of the pictures in here that they'd like."

I asked him, "Why have you got such a big scrapbook as that?"

He said, "Oh, when the Iowa was recommissioned, both San Francisco papers had a picture of the Iowa on the whole top of the front page."

I said, "My God." So I went upstairs, and I got a brown manila envelope, where I had folded up the San Francisco pages, and here was a picture of the Missouri taking up the whole front page from our visit in 1954. So I told my wife, "The next time you go to the Brentano's bookstore, get me one of those great big memory books like that."

Claudia had bought Smeddy this scrapbook to put those things in. He turned over his scrapbook, and he showed me a letter on White House stationery: "Dear Captain Smedberg: The newspapers allege that you made a statement on the commissioning of the Iowa that you commanded the biggest ship afloat. Unless you retract this statement forthwith, drastic action will be taken." Signed, you know who.‡

Well, this was a few months after President Truman had written a letter to the musical editor of The Washington Post named Hume, calling him a son of a bitch for saying that Margaret couldn't sing.§ So Smeddy took a gander at this thing, and he wasn't real sure

---

* Rear Admiral William R. Smedberg III, USN, was superintendent of the Naval Academy from March 1956 to June 1958. His oral history is in the Naval Institute collection.
† As a captain, Smedberg was the commanding officer when the USS Iowa (BB-61) was recommissioned 25 August 1951 after having been reactivated from mothballs for Korean War duty.
‡ "You know who" was President Harry S Truman, whose daughter Margaret had christened the Missouri in 1944.
§ President Truman's daughter sang a concert on 5 December 1950 at Constitution Hall in Washington. Music critic Paul Hume of The Washington Post wrote a scathing review, whereupon Truman responded with a handwritten letter to Hume, describing the physical punishment he would inflict if the two met.

whether he was on firm ground or not, or whether he was in trouble. Then he finally took a look at the register of that time, and he found the White House aide was Dennison, who had commanded the Missouri.* Well, it seems that, actually, the yards that were building these ships did try to stick four inches on here, or something of that kind, to say they built the biggest ship that was ever built. So that mystery was solved for Smeddy.

Q: Well, and President Truman had a personal interest in the ship as well.

Admiral Keith: Oh, sure. He kept it in commission. And this is the reason, I'm convinced, that the Missouri was put out of commission way out in Bremerton. That when the Republicans came in, here was the Missouri running around with a Democratic tag on it from Truman having kept it in commission, when all the others were kept out of commission. So they said, "Okay, we'll fix her." And they put her out in Bremerton.

So I went up there when I was here on duty many years later, and they had 30,000 visitors, when they had to ride the ferry from Seattle, or take a bus from Tacoma, to get to the Missouri in Bremerton, and either one of them was an hour and a half or two-hour trip. And still 30,000 visitors came a year to see the Missouri.

*   *   *

When I was in Destroyer Flotilla Two in Newport, we experimented with the Kaman helicopter.† They had an operating drone helicopter, and we experimented with it for carrying sonobuoys, and for carrying torpedoes out to drop on submarines. I thought that Kaman had a very successful drone system, but it had a barometer-controlled depth control on it, and scientists in the Bureau of Aeronautics said that barometric pressure, when you're that close to the surface, limited control up and down over the waves, and you'd lose too many. So they insisted that we have a radio altimeter, and it never was completely successful, although in the demonstration for the President, we located a

---

* Captain Robert L. Dennison, USN, commanded the Missouri from 2 April 1947 to 23 January 1948. He was then naval aide to the President from 1948 to 1953.
† This was Keith's first billet as a flag officer.

submarine with a drone helicopter out here in 1963, and we dropped sonar buoys.* A submarine sent up a flare saying that we had him pinned down, and he surfaced right where we said he was.

So now, when you read Red Storm Rising or something of this kind, you see the towed sonar array, which we were experimenting with and hoped would be available to us in the fleet.† Now that's the main means of doing business in submarine detection. Helicopter detection is another primary means. These were things that we were looking for and playing with, and there are a great many more of them that you see today.

*   *   *

I want to tell you a story about Don Felt.‡ When he was commander in the Pacific and I had the naval base at Subic Bay, I got a letter from him. He said, "Dear Keith, I am coming out to Subic Bay, and I want to see you and hear about the base and its developments. I don't want any normal briefing. I've heard all the normal briefings I want. I want to know what your problems are."

Well, Subic Bay consisted then of an ammunition depot, an air station, supply depot, a repair station, a naval station, and my base staff. I invited all the commanding officers of those activities to my quarters for lunch. I met Admiral Felt at Cubi airport about quarter to 12:00, and we started for my quarters, which were some four or five miles away and up on a series of hills back of the bay at Subic. As we approached the road leading off to the naval station, with my road going straight through the T, a fire truck, big and red, pulled out in front of us and dashed down the road until it came to the first hill.

There were big double white lines along the road, and Admiral Felt's car, with me in it, and our chauffeur--and with the admiral's four-star flags flying--was forced to follow this truck. Well, it was all right on the level, but when we got to the hill, the truck went into low gear, and finally into high dudgeon before it could finally get up that hill--or at least we

---

* This is a reference to President John F. Kennedy's visit to Navy ships when Vice Admiral Keith was Commander First Fleet in 1963.
† Tom Clancy's novel Red Storm Rising (New York: G. P. Putnam's, 1986) was published shortly before this interview. It contains the scenario for a wide-ranging world conflict.
‡ Admiral Harry D. Felt, USN, served as Commander in Chief Pacific from 31 July 1958 to 30 June 1964.

were in high dudgeon. Then it got started off down that next hill, and went sailing up the next one a little ways, then went through the same performance, with us having to practically stop behind. When we got to the top of the second hill, we were nearly home, and I said, "Admiral, you saw that fire truck pull out in front of us as you were coming along the road."

He said, "Yes, I did."

I said, "It was there on purpose, Admiral. You wanted to know about my problems, and my problem now is, sir, that that fire truck was purchased by CinCPac's universal purchasing agency. And the fire trucks are purchased by the United States Army, and it was bought to run over the center part of the United States. It was bought in Chicago somewhere, no hills or anything to worry about. Now, my worry is, sir, since your fire marshal in CinCPac says that I don't need a fire station up here, and they've made me close it up, and it's two and two-eighths miles down to the fire station at the base, and they say if there's one within two and a half miles, that you don't need one any closer than that. My great problem out here, though, sir, is with CinCPac on board, if my quarters catch on fire while you're there, you're going to burn to death before that goddamn truck can get up the hill." [Laughter]

The next time I got a letter from Admiral Felt, he said, "Dear Taylor."

Q: A little friendlier this time.

Admiral Keith: As I told you, earlier he had said, "Dear Keith." So we've been friends ever since.

Q: So did you get another fire truck?

Admiral Keith: Really, it's so long ago, I've forgotten, but I know I got my fire station back.

*   *   *

I'm very happy that I didn't make the decision to be a lawyer, but I did have a good deal of experience in the Navy's legal line. A lot of it came after we switched over from the old Courts and Boards to the new manuals. Before I went to the Missouri, I was chief of staff to Admiral Hartman, Commander Destroyers Atlantic, and he had general court-martial authority for all the New England area.[*] So I read a good many courts every month. I reviewed all the big courts and the summary courts-martial and took them in to him for signature.

Later I went to the Philippines, and there I had general court-martial authority for the Philippines. One interesting thing there was amusing. Because when I was a squadron commander in destroyers, I had had occasion to research old court-martial orders, looking for an authority to disapprove a court that I wanted to get off the record. A sailor man was accused of stealing government whiskey from a radar picket ship that was in my squadron.[†] The Navy authorized captains of radar picket ships transiting the Panama Canal on their way out to the picket stations off Okinawa to fortify the government ration of rum to the extent that when they'd had a rough day on the picket line, they could issue a tot of rum to the crew from their own stores. The skippers were allowed to buy it out of bond in Panama at their own expense.

After the war, some of the picket ships hadn't gotten really broken in out there and hadn't been damaged on the picket stations, and the captains had a good deal of liquor left over. One of them tried to recoup, in this particular instance. When his officers were going ashore at some little port somewhere after the war--along the China coast, or the Philippines, or wherever they might be--he would let them buy a bottle of booze. He wouldn't let them drink on board ship, but they could take it ashore with them and have a drink.

Well, he kept this supply locked up in the government liquor locker, and the sailors knew where it was. On Thanksgiving night, they went down, and they took some of the liquor, and they were charged with stealing government property. It was pretty evident it was the captain's property; it wasn't government property. I didn't want all the little young

---

[*] Rear Admiral Charles C. Hartman, USN.
[†] As a captain, Keith commanded Destroyer Squadron Three in early 1946.

eager lawyers that had come into the Navy during the war to get ahold of this bungling of justice; they'd recommended him for some severe punishment. So I was looking for somebody to disapprove the court and get it off the record. I finally found out from court-martial orders, after two weeks' research back in Saipan, that if the evidence of a co-conspirator was used to convict a man who was pleading not guilty, and if the evidence given by the co-conspirator freely, if he wasn't tried first--the co-conspirator that was giving the evidence--that they couldn't use his evidence against the man who they were going to try to convict under this so-called pal's evidence. So I disapproved the court.

When we got out to the Philippines a number of years later, a couple of sailors and a couple of Filipinos stole an LST. They took it outside the bay of Subic, and they took the engine out of it. A few days later, we found the hulk, with no engines in it, drifting somewhere off of Subic. Well, somehow or other, the naval intelligence people got on the trail of these two sailors, and finally they got a confession out of one of them. I had a staff of seven lawyers working for me; the senior one was a captain. He came in one afternoon, bringing two general courts-martial for me to sign, ordering them tried by a general court-martial. I read them over, and I looked up at him, and I said, "Which one of these are you going to try first?"

He said, "Whichever court's ready. It doesn't make any difference."

I said, "I'm not real sure that you are correct legally on this point. Would you check to see whether or not you can use the evidence of a co-conspirator against his co-conspirator, unless he's been tried first."

He looked at me in almost amazement, and he took the courts and went out. He came back two days later and said, "I'll be damned if I know how you knew it, but that's right." [Laughter] So that established me as a legal eagle. I think I've held my family tradition.

Q: What was the distinction you were drawing between a guy stealing a captain's whiskey, as opposed to government whiskey?

Admiral Keith: Well, it was taken out of a liquor locker, and the captain had bought the whiskey and paid for it; it was his whiskey.

Q: But theft is theft. Why is that any less culpable?

Admiral Keith: Because he was charged with stealing government property.

Q: So the charge was improperly drawn.

Admiral Keith: Sure. That was. But that never worried me very much. It was the charge of stealing government property, which is a much more serious offense than stealing.

Q: I see.

Admiral Keith: And the captain would never have accused anybody of stealing his whiskey, because he wasn't supposed to have it on board ship.

Q: I see.

Admiral Keith: But he thought that breaking into this locker and taking this whiskey was bad, that it was bad for the command. He didn't really research his problem too far, and he didn't have good legal advice. This is a problem that you run into, where you don't have a lawyer around to check what you're doing. It goes back to what I was saying, that if your subordinates don't give of their knowledge, you can make mistakes.

But we were in a situation then where we'd had the new legal system, I think, foisted on us, because in World War II, when we established courts-martial ashore to try deserters and AOL cases, they were mostly manned by recalled retirees. I don't know whether your knowledge goes back to the fact that when we established the selection law in 1934, we had "retained and best fitted" lieutenants in the Navy. A lot of those retained lieutenants were brought back as lieutenant commanders in the war, and a lot of the lieutenant commanders who were under the previous to 1934 system were brought back as lieutenant commanders or commanders in the Navy. A lot of those who had no recent experience in the Navy were assigned to take up these shore billets and let other people go to sea.

The reaction to their arrogance as members of courts-martial, that, "I know this man's guilty, and we're going to hang him," regardless of any evidence to the contrary. The young lawyers just out of law school, that riled the hell out of them. The young lawyers that saw this going on were the ones that got us into trouble under the old Courts and Boards.

I served on lots of courts and boards in the days when we were at sea, and I never saw any fairer system than that for trial. It was certainly as fair as our courts are today in the civilian world. People spent a lot of time. My evidence to you of spending two weeks researching one court-martial--true, I was looking for something in particular, but when court-martial orders came out, I read them all. When I was an ensign, on a summary court-martial, I was alert to what had happened and the decision made in court-martial. You could turn to the index and find in the old court-martial orders similar cases to the one that you had before you. People made an effort to be just, be fair, and to provide assistance to the sailor that was in trouble. I've defended many of them.

The mistake was in using people who were doing their duty, but really not with any great love of the service that they were serving. That love of your service has got to be an influence on your actions. You don't do anything that's going to really hurt, if you can avoid it, if you love it.

Q: It sounds as if there were people who weren't really capable to do much more.

Admiral Keith: Well, it's true that they filled billets that needed to be filled, and you had a great deal of trouble with people who didn't want to go back to the war zone, who missed their ship. They were guilty, but other people, who fell into the clutches of the law for some other reason, were probably given pretty rough treatment. I've talked to people who served from the legal profession in the Navy during the war, and they were pretty upset about it. Their evidence before Congress was pretty bitter about the naval system of justice under the Courts and Boards.

* * *

I'm just about run out of talk. I do want to talk about two things. One is two opportunities I had in my life, once when I was base commander at Subic Bay, and once when I was the United Nations representative in Korea, to sit with our ambassadors overseas in a decision-making process, to make a recommendation to Washington, to the State Department and the Navy Department, as to what policies should be pursued in matters pertinent to the times.

When Ambassador Chip Bohlen was in the Philippines, we were talking about the Philippine demands that they have a commander at our bases and that they be the commanding officer.* In addition to that, they said that offenders caught in the Philippines should be tried in Philippine courts and not turned over to the Navy or the Air Force or the Army for military punishment.

We had wonderful examples to show that the Philippine courts were very, very slow, that getting to trial was more a question of whom you knew and how much you could put into their palms behind the table or behind their back, to get their case tried, than it was following an orderly procession of dispensing justice. So we made recommendations to Washington, strongly opposing the State Department's statement that they were going to recommend that they return to Philippine jurisdiction all of our possessions out there.

This was turned down by the State Department over the Secretary of State's signature. Mr. Bohlen told me that he was certain that the Secretary of State had never seen his recommendation. He was pretty irate about it.

* * *

I had lots of dealings with Congress through those years. They always gave you an ear, and they gave you intelligent questions. When they set a date, they usually were there and kept it. I'm making this point because things had changed by the time I got to be an admiral and went there as OP-01R for reserves in 1959, and I guess I went more frequently

---

* Charles E. Bohlen was U.S. ambassador to the Philippines, 1957-59.

as O1R because the reserves were always something that the Congress was interested in. I would go up there as an admiral and cool my heels for an hour and a half, even two hours, waiting for one representative to come in, so that I could read what I had to say into the record. I don't think anybody in the subcommittee or the committee that I appeared before ever read it. Some recent graduate of Missouri or Princeton or MIT, or wherever he came from, could take a political science course and sit down as an executive secretary or something for that committee, and he would write a report, and that's what they read, and they never really sat down and looked at the reports. I think that's true today.

I think the change in the congressional actions is absolutely astounding within my memory, and I'm talking about 1959. You'd have to talk to people today to find out whether they think they're getting what they have to say, their reasoning, truly before a committee. You get it if it's on television, when it's Iran or something of this kind, but the basic day-in and day-out matters that have to be decided by Congress, I don't think that they're getting the story put before them anymore. They're just too damn busy getting reelected for them to have any time to do what business we elect them to do. Now that I've delivered myself of that diatribe, I'll go to something else.

*   *   *

In the early '60s I was commander of the destroyer force.* Having started in and enjoyed the destroyers, as the youngest and the most inexperienced, and gone through to gunnery officer, to assistant engineering officer, to exec, to division commander, squadron commander, to commander of the antisubmarine group in the destroyer flotilla, and finally to command of the whole force, with 200-some ships under me in the Pacific, I think that's the highlight of my whole life. It was a chance that I had to put some ideas into work. We did have lots of ideas, and we did work on those things that we see in the fleet today.

Following that thought, we brought the first NTDS system into the fleet, into King

---

* In 1960, as a rear admiral, Keith became Commander Cruiser-Destroyer Force Pacific Fleet.

and into Mahan, and the carrier Oriskany.* I had a chief of staff then who had had command of one of the early missile ships. In talking with him, he told me once, "We relied on the manufacturer to keep our missiles going. It was so when I took command of the ship, and it continued to be so." He said, "The manufacturer's representative in the local area was a plank owner on the ship. He'd been there longer than any sailor. He came aboard in the morning as a civilian, he saluted the colors. He knew practically everybody on board by their first names, and he was known by everybody in the crew. He said, "We're bringing a new weapon system into the fleet, and I think we ought to make the Navy sailor man stand up on his hind legs and operate. I think we ought to deploy them just as fast as we can get them ready and get them out to the Western Pacific."

Well, we did just that. They fired their missiles, they maintained the equipments, they did everything that they were asked to do, and they did it without ever asking for anything but spare parts. Again, we had to fly spare parts out, because we robbed Peter to pay Paul. But spare parts is an entirely different subject.

We brought them back from their deployment. I flew out and boarded the ships, and AirPac went out to the Oriskany.

The Mahan was commanded by Bill Busik.† I know he was the first commander, and I think he deployed. They had done as much as anybody could do to put a new weapon system into place in the fleet and to learn how to operate it.

* * *

Admiral Don Felt made a statement once which I've quoted, and I'll quote it again. During one of the forays, or uprisings, or flurries in the Vietnamese War, when he was commander of the Pacific, he was questioned by newspapermen in Hawaii about what he was doing with his forces to handle the situation. Admiral Felt said, "Gentlemen, I have

---

* For a description of NTDS, the Navy tactical data system, see Norman Friedman, U.S. Naval Weapons (Annapolis: Naval Institute Press, 1985), pages 142-146. The King (DLG-10) and Mahan (DLG-11) were guided missile frigates; the Oriskany (CVA-34) was an aircraft carrier.
† Commander William S. Busik, USN, was the first commanding officer when the Mahan was commissioned 25 August 1960.

been dealt a very strong hand. Each pip on those cards represents a ship. I have them together, and I know what I'm going to do with them, but it is no time to talk about it now. The time now is to plan, to dispose my forces appropriately to meet the situation with which I'm faced. And when it comes time, I will play my hand. Until then it's my business." Or words to that effect. I'm not quoting him verbatim, but that's so true.

In talking to ships on commissionings, such as the Towers, when I was the commissioning speaker, I used Admiral Felt's example there.* But there I made the engine room, the repair parties, the radiomen, the signalmen, the gunners, everybody, a card in that deck--the cooks, the water tenders. And every one of them has to be ready to be played, or that damn hand can be ruined, and you can go sit right quick. Felt made a beautiful analysis, to me, of what we have in the Navy and had as a team--a deck of cards, that if one of them is missing, it's no good.

*   *   *

When I went to Korea, I found out--and I'm not sure how I learned it, but I did learn it--that our ambassador in Moscow and the Red Chinese ambassador in Moscow were meeting in Warsaw to discuss possible improvements of Chinese-American relations. Well, this was pretty startling to me, because I was sitting across the table from the Chinese representative on General Han's staff there, two or three times a month. I had been back to Washington to be briefed on my assignment as the U.N. spokesman at Panmunjom, but I was given absolutely no guidelines as to what I could say and what I shouldn't say.† Because you got into a name-calling situation, which all the records show that for nine years before I got there, the arms disagreement had been a vituperative sort of meeting. Anything that you charged in the way of a violation in the armistice, they called you a liar and said that they hadn't done it, but that you had, and that you were trying to say that they did it.

Anyhow, I felt that if I was going to be a U.N. representative there, then I ought to know what the United States's position, vis-a-vis China, was, so that in my wrath I wouldn't say something that would be blown up in the newspapers and turn out to be a stumbling

---

* The guided missile destroyer Towers (DDG-9) was commissioned 6 June 1961 at the Puget Sound Naval Shipyard.
† U.N.--United Nations.

block, minor though it probably would be, to anything that we were trying to accomplish with Red China.

We got an answer back, after the ambassador had made this recommendation, General McAuliffe's and my recommendation that we be briefed, and they said it was very closely held and only those that need to know needed to know. Well, this made the general and Admiral Keith pretty mad, and we wondered who needed to know any more than the man who was talking to the Red as frequently as I was.

So it made Ambassador Berger mad.[*] He went back pretty strongly, but he again said, "That message never got to the Secretary of State." He sent one back saying that he recommended that this message go to no other one than the eyes of the Secretary of State. We got a resumé after that of what was being said in Warsaw by the Moscow ambassador.

When I got back to Washington in '59, from the Philippines, I was very anxious to find out just how many people in the State Department had an ability to answer a message. They don't send them out by direction; they send them out with the Secretary's name signed to them. I found out that they had 23 people in the State Department authorized to sign the Secretary of State's name. That ain't right. So there are too many cooks trying to boil the pot, it seems to me, around the world.

* * *

About this time, I had become an exalted vice admiral, and a year later I was called back to Washington--1963.[†] George Anderson was still CNO, and he said, "I've got a job for you."[‡] He said, "Last year we gave a demonstration for the commander in chief of modern weapon systems in the Atlantic, and nothing worked. He's given us a reprieve, and he's coming out to the Pacific to have a demonstration of a modern weapon systems. And you're to plan it and conduct it, and you can't make any mistakes."

Q: By "commander in chief," you mean President Kennedy.

---

[*] Samuel D. Berger was U.S. ambassador to the Republic of Korea.
[†] In 1962 Keith was promoted to the rank of vice admiral when he took command of the First Fleet, based on the West Coast.
[‡] Admiral George W. Anderson, Jr., USN, served as Chief of Naval Operations from 1 August 1961 to 1 August 1963

Admiral Keith: That's right. He was pretty upset in the Atlantic. I don't know anything about what they did, but I had a boss out here named John Sides, who was known as Savvy, for good reason.[*]

Q: And he was a missile man.

Admiral Keith: He was a wonderful boss. We talked of plans. I gave him my recommendation, and we agreed that the most interesting thing we had to demonstrate was the NTDS system. He said, "See what you can do."

So with Paul Masterton's assistance, we went to work.[†] We decided that what we were going to do was to station the King and the Mahan well away from the Oriskany. And we were going to take the President on board the Oriskany, and that the King and the Mahan were to report from their various stations that there were bandits. We would rig it to the point that we would have the NTDS give us a solution for each of the weapon systems that we had.

We would have a head-on air attack, where we used the ahead-firing weapons. We would have a tail chase, where we would use the stern-chase Sidewinder. We would use one where they had come through and the screen was going to have to take them under missile fire, and that we would fire a beam-rider, and we would fire a seeker. Those were our weapon systems; they were the most modern things we had.

We decided that the President would be seated in the Oriskany's CIC, that he would see these decisions made, designate, "You will fire the seeker," "You will fire the Sidewinder," and so forth. Then the scene would shift, and we'd put him out to see the results of this attack. He would be seated on the deck of the Kitty Hawk. The resulting

---

[*] Admiral John H. Sides, USN, served as Commander in Chief Pacific Fleet, 30 August 1960 to 30 September 1963.
[†] Rear Admiral Paul Masterton, USN, served as Commander Carrier Division One in 1962-63.

meeting of the weapon systems and the target would be within his vision, and he would have a play-by-play account on the loudspeaker, telling him what was happening.

Before we talk about the results, let me mention a few of the problems that came along. To ensure the safety of the President of the United States, no intercept could be made until after the attacking missile or plane had crossed the bow of the President's flagship. The explosion would occur going away from him, so that there would be no danger of his being damaged. The White House had to come out and see all of the places that he was to go, and they said he couldn't go down the three steps into the CIC on the Oriskany because of a bad back. This, to me, vitiated the whole concept that we had, and I got on a plane and went back to Washington.

George Anderson told me he'd made an appointment for me to go and talk to Shepherd at the White House and the two civilians that had made this decision.[*] The CNO was not going to use whatever influence he had at the White House to fight this battle; that it was mine, and I had to do it. So I went and kept my appointment at the White House and told them that what we had tried to do was design something that would give the President a real insight into the basic problem that you were faced with raiding aircraft or missiles, and the methods that the Congress had provided to handle it. I said that unless he could see where the decisions were made in the Oriskany, then what he saw on board the Kitty Hawk would have no meaning.

We had deployed these three ships, and the sailormen had learned and carried out their learning to make these effective weapon systems in the modern Navy. I said that it was our belief that they were entitled to demonstrate their art and their skills to the commander in chief. They hemmed and hawed. I finally said, "Well, the press knows that I've come back on this business, and they're going to want to know what happened. You don't want me to have to be truthful and tell them that the President is too infirm or too uninterested to see what good American youth has done for them." This is what I said to Shepherd. And I got the President on board the Oriskany. [Laughter]

---

[*] Captain Tazewell T. Shepherd, Jr., USN, was President Kennedy's naval aide.

Well, we sat out at sea and were watching television of his speech over at San Diego State University, before he went to the Marine Corps Recruit Depot to have luncheon. A helicopter was to carry him. He stepped back, bumped his head on the door going into the thing. I said, "Oh, my God. He's hurt his back again. We are in trouble. Stand by to get calls, to get this show on the road in a hurry, or to cancel it."

Sure enough, they wanted to speed it up. You know, we brought this whole thing to fruition one hour earlier. Every intercept was made. By the time we had the missiles going, they could see the airplanes fly by and shoot their missiles, and they saw them hit and saw the target drones go in the water. The missile was a beam-rider, and by the time we fired it, afternoon clouds off California had come into being, and you couldn't see from the Kitty Hawk.[*] But my chief of staff, Walter Curtis, was over on my flagship, and he called in and said, "You got an intercept."[†]

We announced that we had a report from other ships that we had an intercept. The governor of California, Brown, and everybody started tittering.[‡] The congressmen that were there were saying, "We can't see it, but you hit it, huh?. All right." Well, the clouds were up at about 20,000 feet, and while they were still tittering, here came the drone down, in flames, circling down, floating down, and all at once, out of the ozone, came the seeker. Just before that drone hit the water--BANG!--it hit it again. So when they said, "Don't make any mistakes," we didn't.

We flew the drone helicopter, which was a new weapon system. We had it contact a submarine, and we brought the submarine to the surface right alongside the Kitty Hawk, so that the President could see the sonar buoys go in and have it say that this is a contact, and then drop an echo to make them surface. They came up right in view of the President.

Sure enough, he had a masseur along on his trip, and he said he would not come to dinner. He didn't want to see any night flying, so he went to his room, and the masseurs worked on his back. But his room on the Kitty Hawk, where he was going to spend the night, was right alongside of one of those catwalks outside, and he came out of there with

---

[*] President Kennedy's visits to the Oriskany and Kitty Hawk were on 6 June 1963.
[†] Captain Walter L. Curtis, USN.
[‡] Edmund G. "Pat" Brown served as governor of California from 1959 to 1966.

his Secret Service man. They walked up on deck when the Kitty Hawk was flying planes that were going to be used in the demonstration for him over in the desert the next day at Inyokern. There he was, standing behind the blast shield, with a plane on the catapult right in front of him. The safety observer was a young sailor. He ran out and grabbed the President and pulled him into the shack there in the bridge area, and got him out of there. The Secret Service man was looking around at all the screening vessels with the lights on. He turned around, and the President was gone. He practically beat his hands bloody, trying to get through the door, which the sailor had banged shut.

The President heard these planes going off, and that's the reason he'd come up. He had said he didn't want to see them, so we were shooting the planes off. We had saved the one elevator on the Kitty Hawk for the President's use. Nobody else could ride in it all the time he was on board. But the little sailor didn't know anything about an elevator; he never even knew there was an elevator on the ship. So the President asked him how he could see this night flying. He said, "Go up on the bridge, Mr. President. The captain's up there, and you can watch it with him."

He said, "Where is that?"

"Up that ladder, three decks up."

Q: Where were you?

Admiral Keith: I was back on my flagship. Sides was on board the Kitty Hawk.

The President's people had told us he couldn't go down those two steps on the Oriskany, but he climbed all these steps up to the bridge. To tell you that everything went right, that seaman had savvy enough to call the bridge and say, "Captain, the President's on his way up to watch the night flying." The captain went down to the flag bridge, one deck down, and met him, took him over, put him in a seat over there. He picked up the thing and recalled all his planes that he had in the air, had them land on board, take off again. We had wanted to show him night flying, we thought he'd like to see it, but he said he wouldn't have time to see it. So we had released the planes and started flying them off. But old Spin

Epes, he brought them all back in.* You know, strange thing. Spin Epes was selected for admiral the next year. [Laughter]

*   *   *

I ended my naval career in January 1964, when I turned over command of the First Fleet. As part of that ceremony, I invited Chief Fire Controlman Suturowski, who had been my fire control chief on the USS Aylwin, when we were beset with the first automatic 5-inch guns controlled by Thyratron II. He knew his job, he got it done, and he was one of many most capable enlisted people who had served with me. He was retired here in San Diego, and I asked him to sit in the front row at my retirement ceremony, representing the men that I had served with and who helped me so much.

I had Lieutenant Commander Elmer Hurst, who I first knew when he put me through sound school before I went to take command of the Nicholas in '43.† He subsequently served with me in the training group in Pearl Harbor. He was one of the ablest instructors I encountered. He got his ideas across, made his points, no fuss, no bother, but you learned from Elmer Hurst. He was a lieutenant commander when I saw him last; he was a lieutenant when I saw him first. He sat in the front row as a representative of the officers that I had served with.

You feel some satisfaction in looking back on your career. I think I said to you yesterday that I told a young man, who said he wasn't sure he wanted to be a naval officer, that no young man was ever really sure of what he wanted to do. There are too many examples of people that studied this, did something else.

Those two words come back to me in this very happy time for me, in talking about my life in the Navy, and I can say that my career was a very satisfying and satisfactory one to have lived in the Navy.

Thank you.

Q: Thank you, Admiral.

---

* Captain Horace H. Epes, USN, was commanding officer of the Kitty Hawk (CVA-63).
† Lieutenant Commander Elmer C. Hurst, USN (Ret.)

Index To

Reminiscences of

Vice Admiral Robert Taylor Scott Keith

U.S. Navy (Retired)

Admiralty Islands
    Members of the Army's First Cavalry Division ate bountifully while visiting the destroyer Nicholas (DD-449) in the Admiralties in 1944, 69

Aitape, New Guinea
    Fire support by the destroyer Nicholas (DD-449) during the U.S. landings in April 1944, 68-69

Alcoholic Beverages
    In 1939 the commandant of the Mare Island Navy Yard was concerned about excess drinking by sailors on liberty in Vallejo, California, 47-48; courts-martial of Navy men shortly after World War II for allegedly stealing government whiskey from a radar picket ship, 121-123

Ammunition
    The USS Nitro (AE-2) traveled widely in the mid-1930s while transporting ammunition for fleet use, 27-28, 30-31

Amphibious Warfare
    The Base Force supervised amphibious landing exercises in 1937, 43

Anderson, Admiral George W., Jr., USN (USNA, 1927)
    As CNO in 1963, directed the First Fleet to put on a weapons demonstration for President John F. Kennedy, 129-131

Andrews, Vice Admiral Adolphus, USN (USNA, 1901)
    Commanded the Hawaiian Detachment of the U.S. Fleet in 1939-40, 49

Antiair Warfare
    Use of drones during antiaircraft practice by U.S. Fleet ships in 1939, 45-46; destroyers of the Hawaiian Detachment conducted a target practice against drones in 1941, 53-54, 60

Antisubmarine Warfare
    In November 1944 the destroyer Nicholas (DD-449) sank the Japanese submarine I-38, which was armed with Kaiten torpedoes, 69-73; experiments with a drone helicopter in the late 1950s, 118-119; drone helos were part of a First Fleet firepower demonstration in 1963, 132

Argonne, USS (AS-10)
    Served as flagship for Commander Base Force, U.S. Fleet, in the late 1930s, 39, 44-45

Arizona, USS (BB-39)
    Had a poor reputation among Naval Academy graduates in the late 1920s, 3-4, 13; cruised to Puerto Rico with President Herbert Hoover on board in 1931, 13; Commander Thaddeus Thomson was difficult and demanding as executive officer of

the ship in the early 1930s, 13-16; role of the officers of the deck, 16-17; firing of target practice by the 14-inch turrets in the early 1930s, 18-20

Army, U.S.
Members of the First Cavalry Division ate bountifully while visiting the destroyer Nicholas (DD-449) in 1944, 69

Army Air Corps, U.S.
In 1941 many of the pilots stationed near Pearl Harbor were deployed elsewhere in Hawaii, 50

Athletics
Competition among various ship teams in the 1930s, 41-42

Aylwin, USS (DD-355)
Overhauled at Mare Island Navy Yard in 1939, 47; crew on liberty in Vallejo, California, 47-48; was part of the Hawaiian Detachment sent out from the West Coast in late 1939, 49-50, 52; was among a group of destroyers that conducted a target practice against drones in 1941, 53-54, 60; in the late 1930s, the executive officer, Lieutenant Commander William S. Parsons, devised a tactic for night search, 93-94

Barr, Dr. Stringfellow
As president of St. John's College in Annapolis during World War II, resisted strenuously when the Naval Academy conducted a study on the feasibility of putting a Naval Reserve training unit at his school, 65-67

Base Force, U.S. Fleet
Rear Admiral Carleton Watts as force commander in the late 1930s, 37; supervision of shore patrol in the areas where the fleet operated, 38-39, 41-43, involvement in amphibious exercises in 1937, 43; exercises in fueling at sea in the 1930s, 43-44; role of the USS Argonne (AS-10) as flagship, 44-45

Batista, Fulgencio
Role of the U.S. Special Service Squadron when the Batista regime seized power in Cuba in 1933, 22-26

Beardall, Rear Admiral John R., USN (USNA, 1908)
Served as superintendent of the Naval Academy during World War II, 63, 65

Boat Racing
Heavy competition among ships' teams in the late 1930s, 42; Russell S. Callow was crew coach at the Naval Academy in the 1950s, 113-114

Bohlen, Charles E.
As U.S. ambassador to the Philippines in the late 1950s, was involved in negotiations about Filipino jurisdiction in legal cases, 125

Boone, Rear Admiral Walter F., USN (USNA, 1921)
As Naval Academy superintendent in the mid-1950s, he investigated a case in which a midshipman was accused of cheating, 114-116

Brazil
Visited by President-elect Herbert Hoover on board the battleship Utah (BB-31) in December 1928, 7-8

Bryan, Lieutenant Louis A., USN (USNA, 1932)
Served as temporary executive officer of the destroyer Cushing (DD-376) in 1940, 58; was exec of the destroyer Duncan (DD-485) when she sank off Guadalcanal in 1942, 59

Bureau of Naval Personnel
Disposal of surplus property after World War II, 76; installation of Naval Reserve training armories throughout the country shortly after World War II, 77

Burke, Admiral Arleigh A., USN (USNA, 1923)
Served as Commander Cruiser Division Six during a midshipman training cruise in 1954, 103; reviewed a Naval Academy disciplinary case while CNO in the mid-1950s, 115

Callow, Russell S.
Served as crew coach at the Naval Academy in the 1950s, 113-114

Caribbean
The battleship Arizona (BB-39) cruised to Puerto Rico with President Herbert Hoover on board in 1931, 13; role of the Special Service Squadron operating in the region in the early 1930s, 21-26

Chandler, Vice Admiral Alvin Duke, USN (Ret.) (USNA, 1923)
Became president of William & Mary University in the early 1950s, 85

Cherbourg, France
The battleship Missouri (BB-63) visited the port during a midshipman training cruise in July 1954, 97-98, 101, 104

Christie, Ensign Carl G., USN (USNA, 1929)
Was involved in an amusing incident during a captain's inspection of a bunk room in the battleship Florida (BB-30) in the late 1920s, 7-8

Churchill, Sir Winston
British Prime Minister who exchanged greetings with the commanding officer of the battleship Missouri (BB-63) in July 1954, 97-98

Coaling Ship
    The battleship <u>Texas</u> (BB-35) burned coal until her modernization in the mid-1920s, 2

Columbia University, New York, New York
    Dwight Eisenhower was president of the university when it played the Naval Academy in football in 1950, 83-85

Communications
    The ammunition ship <u>Nitro</u> (AE-2) experienced some discrepancies while sending coded messages in the mid-1930s, 29-30

Congress, U.S.
    Keith had to deal with congressmen during World War II when St. John's College complained about a perceived takeover from the Naval Academy, 65-66; complaint by a congressman in the early 1950s about individuals dropped by the service academies because of low aptitude marks, 90-91; concern in the mid-1950s about a Naval Academy midshipman accused of cheating, 114-116; shabby treatment of Keith when he was Assistant Chief of Naval Operations (Naval Reserve) in 1959-60, 125-126

Cornell University, Ithaca, New York
    Interaction with the Naval Academy in the early 1950s, 85, 88-89

Courts-Martial
    Trials of Navy men shortly after World War II for allegedly stealing government whiskey from a radar picket ship, 121-123; trial of individuals for stealing an LST in the Philippines in the late 1950s, 122; Keith's view on the caliber of people who administered the Navy's legal system over the years, 123-125

Creesy, Captain Andrew E., USMC (USNA, 1918)
    Commanded the Marine detachment in the cruiser <u>Richmond</u> (CL-9) when she was flagship of the Special Service Squadron in the early 1930s, 24

Cruiser-Destroyer Force, U.S. Pacific Fleet
    Arrival of the first NTDS-equipped ships in the early 1960s, 126-128

Cuba
    Role of the U.S. Special Service Squadron when the Batista regime seized power in 1933, 22-26; advent of liberty for U.S. sailors, 42-43

<u>Cushing</u>, USS (DD-376)
    Conducted experiments with life rafts in the Hawaii area in 1941, 56-57; officers on board in 1940-41, 58

Damage Control
    Keith studied the subject while a student at the Postgraduate School in the mid-1930s, 32-33; damage control training during battle problems conducted in the Hawaiian

Detachment in 1939-40, 52-53; the destroyer Turner (DD-834) demonstrated damage control equipment during public visiting of the ship in Washington, D.C., in the autumn of 1945, 75-76

Del Valle, Major Pedro A., USMC (USNA, 1915)
Served on the staff of Commander Special Service Squadron during the sergeants' revolt in Cuba in 1933, 23-24

Denfeld, Rear Admiral Louis E., USN (USNA, 1912)
As Assistant Chief of Naval Personnel in World War II, sent Keith to talk to Congress about the relationship between the Naval Academy and St. John's College, 65-66

Dennison, Rear Admiral Robert L., USN (USNA, 1923)
Served as naval aide to President Harry S Truman from 1948 to 1953, 6-7, 117-118

Destroyer Flotilla Two
Experiments in the late 1950s with a drone helicopter for ASW, 118-119

Disciplinary Matters
As Naval Academy superintendent in the mid-1950s, Rear Admiral Walter F. Boone investigated a case in which a midshipman was accused of cheating, 114-116; courts-martial of Navy men shortly after World War II for allegedly stealing government whiskey from a radar picket ship, 121-123; courts-martial of individuals for stealing an LST in the Philippines in the late 1950s, 122; Keith's view on the caliber of people who administered the Navy's legal system over the years, 123-125

Doolin, Lieutenant Edward H., USN (USNA, 1920)
Proficiency in celestial navigation while serving in the battleship Utah (BB-31) in the late 1920s, 11

Drones
Use of during antiaircraft practice by U.S. Fleet ships in 1939, 45-46; destroyers of the Hawaiian Detachment conducted a target practice against drones in 1941, 53-54, 60; experiments in the late 1950s with a drone helicopter for ASW, 118-119; drone helos were part of a First Fleet firepower demonstration in 1963, 132

Duncan, USS (DD-485)
Sinking of off Guadalcanal in October 1942, 59

Dyer, Vice Admiral George C., USN (Ret.) (USNA, 1919)
Served as a coauthor for a memoir of Admiral J. O. Richardson, published in the 1970s, 54-56

Eddy, Lieutenant Daniel T., USN (USNA, 1927)
Served as flag lieutenant for CinCUS, Admiral J. O. Richardson, in 1940-41, 55-56

Education
During World War II the Naval Academy conducted a study on the feasibility of putting a Naval Reserve training unit at St. John's College in Annapolis, 65-66; concerns about the Naval Academy curriculum in the early 1950s, 88-90

Eisenhower, Dwight D.
The seniority of White House naval aides dropped when he became President in 1953, 6-7; was president of Columbia University when it played the Naval Academy in football in 1950, 83-85; greatly respected the intellect of Navy Captain Edward Hazlett, a life-long friend from his youth, 84-87; the USS Williamsburg (AGC-369) ceased service as the presidential yacht in the early 1950s because Milton Eisenhower convinced his brother Dwight she was an unnecessary luxury, 86

Engineering Plants
Recycling of engineering plant components from the battleship Kentucky (BB-66), which was never completed, 94; characteristics of the plant of the battleship Missouri (BB-63), 94-96

Epes, Captain Horace H., USN
Commanded the aircraft carrier Kitty Hawk (CVA-63) when President John F. Kennedy was on board during a First Fleet firepower demonstration in June 1963, 133-134

Felt, Admiral Harry D., USN (USNA, 1923)
As Commander in Chief Pacific, made an inspection visit to the U.S. naval base at Subic Bay in the Philippines in the late 1950s, 119-120; commented on the use of various tools in the Vietnam War, 127-128

Fire Control
During fleet antiair gunnery practice in 1939, 45-46; use of visual range finders in the late 1930s, 46-47; on board the destroyer Aylwin (DD-355) in 1941, 52; destroyers of the Hawaiian Detachment conducted a target practice against drones in 1941, 53-54, 60; scheme worked out by the destroyer Nicholas (DD-449) in 1943 to fire 5-inch guns at Japanese searchlights, 68

First Fleet, U.S.
Put on an impressive firepower demonstration for President John F. Kennedy in June 1963, 129-134

Fleet Problems
Role of aircraft carriers in the U.S. Navy's Fleet Problem IX in the Panama area in January 1929, 9; value of post-exercise critiques, 9-10

Florida, USS (BB-30)
Amusing incident during a captain's inspection of a bunk room in the ship in the late 1920s, 7-8

Food
    Members of the Army's First Cavalry Division ate bountifully while visiting the destroyer Nicholas (DD-449) in the Admiralty Islands in 1944, 69

Football
    Dwight Eisenhower was president of Columbia University when it played the Naval Academy in football in 1950, 83-85

Forrestel, Lieutenant Commander William J., USN (USNA, 1916)
    Commanded the destroyer Overton (DD-239) during duty with the Special Service Squadron in the early 1930s, 25

France
    The battleship Missouri (BB-63) visited the port of Cherbourg during a midshipman training cruise in July 1954, 97-98, 101, 104

Freeman, Rear Admiral Charles S., USN (USNA, 1900)
    Commanded the battleship Arizona (BB-39) in the early 1930s, 17, 19; commanded the Special Service Squadron in the Caribbean in the mid-1930s, 23, 25-26

Gallery, Lieutenant Daniel V., Jr., USN (USNA, 1921)
    Provided aviation familiarization to new Naval Academy graduates in the late 1920s, 2-3

Germany
    Visited by the battleship Utah (BB-31) during a summer cruise in 1929, 10

Gray, Gordon
    As Assistant Secretary of the Army in the late 1940s, was part of a board that studied the question of whether the National Guard should be federalized, 78-79

Guadalcanal
    The destroyer Duncan (DD-485) was sunk in the Battle of Cape Esperance in October 1942, 59

Guided Missiles
    Used in putting on an impressive First Fleet firepower demonstration for President John Kennedy in June 1963, 130-134

Gunnery--Naval
    Firing of target practice by the battleship Arizona (BB-39) in the early 1930s, 18-20; use of drones during antiaircraft practice by U.S. Fleet ships in 1939, 45-46; destroyers based at Pearl Harbor conducted a target practice against drones in 1941, 53-54, 60; scheme worked out by the destroyer Nicholas (DD-449) in 1943 to fire 5-inch guns at Japanese searchlights, 68; firing of the 16-inch guns of the battleship Missouri (BB-63) in 1954, 107-108; firing of the 14-inch guns of the battleship Texas (BB-35) during night battle practice in the late 1920s, 107-108

Havana, Cuba
Visited by ships of the U.S. Special Service Squadron when the Batista regime seized power in 1933, 24-26

Hawaii
In 1939 the U.S. Fleet established a Hawaiian Detachment based at Pearl Harbor, 49-50, 52-54; in 1950 Captain Samuel Eliot Morison delivered a series of lectures in Hawaii concerning U.S. naval operations in World War II, 50-51

Hawaii, University of
In 1950 Captain Samuel Eliot Morison delivered a series of lectures at the university concerning U.S. naval operations in World War II, 50-51

Hazlett, Captain Edward E., Jr., USN (Ret.) (USNA, 1915)
Was a life-long friend of Dwight Eisenhower, who greatly respected Hazlett's intellect, 84-87

Helicopters
Experiments in the late 1950s with a drone helicopter for ASW, 118-119; drone helos were part of a First Fleet firepower demonstration in 1963, 132

Herbert J. Thomas, USS (DD-833)
Training of crew members in 1945 for possible encounters with Japanese kamikazes, 74-75

Hill, Vice Admiral Harry W., USN (USNA, 1911)
Overhauled the Naval Academy's honor concept while serving as superintendent in the early 1950s, 81-83; declined to attend a Navy-Columbia football game in 1950 because he wasn't invited by Columbia's president, Dwight Eisenhower, 83-84

Hillenkoetter, Lieutenant Roscoe H., USN (USNA, 1920)
Served on the staff of Commander Special Service Squadron during the sergeants' revolt in Cuba in 1933, 23-25

Hoover, Herbert C.
Made a goodwill tour of South America on board the battleships Maryland (BB-46) and Utah (BB-31) after his election as President in 1928, 5-9, 12; introduced to the medicine ball for exercise, 6; skill at public speaking, 8

Hunters Point Naval Shipyard, San Francisco, California
A pilot bringing the battleship Missouri (BB-63) into the shipyard in 1954 did a poor job of judging the current, 109-110

Hurst, Lieutenant Commander Elmer C., USN (Ret.)
Attended Keith's retirement ceremony in 1964 as a representative of the officers with whom Keith had served during his career, 134

I-38 (Japanese Submarine)
   In November 1944 the destroyer Nicholas (DD-449) sank the I-38, which was armed with Kaiten torpedoes, 69-73

Inspections
   Amusing incident during a captain's inspection of a bunk room in the battleship Florida (BB-30) in the late 1920s, 8-9; personnel inspections on board the battleship Missouri (BB-63) in 1954, 95-96; personnel inspections on board the battleship Arizona (BB-39) in the 1930s, 96

Iowa, USS (BB-61)
   When the ship was recommissioned in 1951, her commanding officer heard from President Harry Truman, who challenged the skipper's claim on the size of the ship, 117-118

J. Fred Talbott, USS (DD-156)
   Irregularities on the part of some of the ship's officers while she was part of the Special Service Squadron in the Caribbean in the early 1930s, 25-26

Jackson, Lieutenant Commander William B., Jr., USN (USNA, 1921)
   Commanded the destroyer Cushing (DD-376) in 1941, 56-58

Japanese Navy
   In November 1944 the destroyer Nicholas (DD-449) sank the Japanese submarine I-38, which was armed with Kaiten torpedoes, 69-73

Kaiten Torpedoes
   In November 1944 the destroyer Nicholas (DD-449) sank the Japanese submarine I-38, which was armed with Kaiten torpedoes, 69-73

Kamikazes
   Training of the crew of the destroyer Herbert J. Thomas (DD-833) in 1945 for possible encounters with kamikazes, 74-75

   See also Kaiten Torpedoes

Keith, Vice Admiral Robert T. S., USN (Ret.) (USNA, 1928)
   Parents of, 1-2; boyhood in Virginia in the 1910s and 1920s, 1-2; education of, 2; attended the Naval Academy in the mid-1920s, 2; flight familiarization at Annapolis in 1928, 2-3; served 1928-30 in the battleship Utah (BB-31), 3-12; served 1930-32 in the battleship Arizona (BB-39), 13-20; served 1932-34 in the destroyer Overton (DD-239), 20-27; served 1934-35 in the ammunition ship Nitro (AE-2), 27-31, 109; studied at the Postgraduate School and Naval Observatory, 1935-37, 31-36; wife of, 35-36, 60, 62; served from 1937 to 1939 on the staff of Commander Base Force, 37-47; served 1939-41 as gunnery officer of the destroyer Aylwin (DD-355), 47-50, 52-54; commanded the training force in Hawaii in 1950, 50-52; as executive officer of

the destroyer Cushing (DD-376) in 1941, 56-59; as a company officer from 1941 to 1943 at the Naval Academy, 59-66; children of, 62, 64; grandchildren of, 64; commanded the destroyer Nicholas (DD-449), 1943-45, 67-73; commanded the destroyer Herbert J. Thomas (DD-833) in 1945, 74-75; commanded destroyer divisions in 1945-46, 75-76; served 1946-49 in the Bureau of Naval Personnel, 76-79; duty from 1950 to 1953 as secretary of the Naval Academy's academic board, 80-91; commanded the battleship Missouri (BB-63) for several months in 1954, 92-114; served from 1954 to 1956 as Naval Academy commandant of midshipmen, 114-118; commanded Destroyer Flotilla Two, 1956-57, 119-120; commanded the U.S. naval base at Subic Bay in the Philippines, 1957-59, 119-125; served as Assistant CNO (Naval Reserve), 1959-60, 125-126; commanded Cruiser-Destroyer Force Pacific Fleet, 1960-61, 126-128; as U.N. negotiator in Korea in 1961-62, 128-129; retirement from active duty in 1964, 134

Keith, Captain R. T. S. Jr., USN (USNA, 1958)
Visited the battleship New Jersey (BB-62) at Long Beach in 1984, 106

Keith, Midshipman R. T. S. III, USN (USNA, 1987)
Followed in his father's and grandfather's footsteps by going to the Naval Academy, 64; visited the battleship New Jersey (BB-62) at Long Beach in 1984, 106

Kentucky, (BB-66)
Though the ship was never completed, components from her engineering plant were put to use, 94

Kempff, Rear Admiral Clarence F., USN (USNA, 1897)
As commandant of the Mare Island Navy Yard in 1939 was concerned about excess drinking by sailors on liberty in Vallejo, California, 47-48

Kennedy, John F.
As President in June 1963, witnessed an impressive firepower demonstration put on First Fleet ships off the coast of California, 129-134

King, USS (DLG-10)
Guided missile frigate that in the early 1960s was one of the first ships in the Pacific Fleet equipped with NTDS, 126-127, 130

Kitty Hawk, USS (CVA-63)
Participated in a First Fleet firepower demonstration for President John Kennedy in June 1963, 130-134

Korea-North
Negotiating with the North Koreans was difficult and frustrating for U.N. representatives in the early 1960s, 128-129

Lawrence, Midshipman William P., USN (USNA, 1951)
As president of his Naval Academy class, had a considerable role in devising a new honor concept in the early 1950s, 82-83

Leave and Liberty
Supervision of shore patrol for sailors on liberty in the late 1930s, 38-39, 41-43; in 1939 the commandant of the Mare Island Navy Yard was concerned about excessive drinking by the sailors on liberty in Vallejo, California, 47-48

Libby, Rear Admiral Ruthven E., USN (USNA, 1922)
Embarked in the battleship Missouri (BB-63) as flagship while commanding the midshipman training squadron in 1954, 98-102, 104; demonstrated great skill in maneuvering a formation of ships, 102; was the subject of an editorial tribute on his death in 1986, 103

Life Rafts
The destroyer Cushing (DD-376) conducted experiments with life rafts in the Hawaii area in 1941, 56-57

Lisbon, Portugal
The battleship Missouri (BB-63) visited the port during a midshipman training cruise in 1954, 98-99

Long Beach, California
Operation of the shore patrol when the U.S. Fleet was based there in the late 1930s, 38-39, 41; many people from the area visited the battleship Missouri (BB-63) when she was in Long Beach for a visit in 1954, 110-111

Long Beach Naval Shipyard
Reactivated the battleship Missouri (BB-63) in the mid-1980s, 106-107

Mahan, USS (DLG-11)
Guided missile frigate that in the early 1960s was one of the first ships in the Pacific Fleet equipped with NTDS, 126-127, 130

Mare Island Navy Yard, Vallejo, California
In 1939 the commandant of the yard was concerned about excessive drinking by sailors on liberty in Vallejo, 47-48

Marine Corps, U.S.
Role of Marines as part of the Special Service Squadron operating in the Caribbean in the early 1930s, 21-26

Markland, Commander Henry T., USN (USNA, (1908)
Commanded the ammunition ship Nitro (AE-2) during survey work around Wake Island in the mid-1930s, 28-30

Maryland, USS (BB-46)
  Hosted President-elect Herbert Hoover during part of a goodwill cruise to South America in late 1928, 5; had excellent results during fleet antiaircraft practice in 1939, 46

Maxson, Lieutenant (j.g.) Willis E. III, USN (USNA, 1943)
  Topflight Naval Academy midshipman who was later killed in action during World War II, 64

Medical Problems
  In July 1954 the surgeon of the battleship New Jersey (BB-62) performed an appendectomy on a crewman from the battleship Missouri (BB-63), 100-101

Military Academy, U.S., West Point, New York
  In the early 1950s dropped a cadet who did not fulfill his potential, 91

Miller, Captain Edwin S., USN (USNA, 1933)
  As executive officer at the Naval Academy in the mid1950s, he helped deal with a case in which a midshipman was accused of cheating, 114-116

Missouri, USS (BB-11)
  Received a silver service from the state of Missouri shortly after 1900, 108-109

Missouri, USS (BB-63)
  Handling characteristics in shallow water, 92-95; personnel inspections in 1954, 95-96; repairs to the engineering plant, 96-97; midshipman training cruise to France and Portugal in the summer of 1954, 97-105, 109; transfer of a crewman to the battleship New Jersey (BB-62) for an appendectomy in July 1954, 100-101; inactivation of in 1954, 105-106; recommissioning at San Francisco in 1986, 106-107; firing of the 16-inch guns in 1954, 107-108; description of the captain's mess and silver service, 108-109; a pilot bringing the ship into San Francisco in 1954 did a poor job of judging the current, 109-110; public visiting in West Coast ports in 1954, 110-113; transits of the Panama Canal in 1954 and 1986, 111-112

Moreell, Admiral Ben, CEC, USN
  Headed a commission that formulated Naval Academy expansion plans in the late 1940s, 77-78

Morison, Captain Samuel Eliot, USNR
  In 1950 delivered a series of lectures in Hawaii concerning U.S. naval operations in World War II, 50-51

Morris, Lieutenant (j.g.) Robert L., USN (USNA, 1928)
  Served in destroyers of the Special Service Squadron in the early 1930s, 25-26

NTDS
  See Navy Tactical Data System

National Guard
In the late 1940s a board of assistant service secretaries studied the question of whether the National Guard should be federalized, 78-79

Naval Academy, U.S., Annapolis, Maryland
Commander Thaddeus Thomson was difficult to deal with when he was executive officer in the 1920s, 14; assignment of officers to the executive department in the early 1940s, 59-61; grading of midshipmen in aptitude for the service, 62-64, 90-91; superintendents in the early 1940s, 63; topflight midshipmen in the early 1940s, 64; conducted a study in World War II on the feasibility of putting a Naval Reserve training unit at St. John's College in Annapolis, 64-66; in the late 1940s Admiral Ben Moreell headed a commission that studied expansion plans for the academy, 77-78; difficulty getting naval aviators assigned to the staff in the early 1950s, 80; overhaul of the honor concept when Vice Admiral Harry Hill was superintendent in the early 1950s, 81-83; Dwight Eisenhower was president of Columbia University when it played the Naval Academy in football in 1950, 83-85; midshipmen served as guinea pigs on standardized tests in the early 1950s, 87-88; comparison of curriculum with other universities, 88-90; the battleship Missouri (BB-63) made a midshipman training cruise to France and Portugal in the summer of 1954, 97-105, log; Russell S. Callow as crew coach in the 1950s, 113-114; resolution of a case in the mid-1950s in which a midshipman was accused of cheating, 114-116

Naval Observatory, Washington, D.C.
Work in the mid-1930s in making precise measurements of time for the purpose of celestial navigation, 33-35

Naval Postgraduate School, U.S. Naval, Annapolis, Maryland, and Monterey, California
Closed briefly in the early 1930s so the students could man decommissioned destroyers, 24; instruction in the general line course in the mid-1930s, 31-33, 36; site of a speech by Keith in the early 1960s, 36-37

Naval Reserve
During World War II the Naval Academy conducted a study on the feasibility of putting a Naval Reserve training unit at St. John's College in Annapolis, 65-66; installation of Naval Reserve training armories throughout the country shortly after World War II, 77

Navigation
Practice in celestial navigation in the battleship Utah (BB-31) in the late 1920s, 11-12; the ammunition ship Nitro (AE-2) did survey work around Wake Island in the mid-1930s, 28-29; in the mid-1930s the Naval Observatory in Washington, D.C., made precise measurements of time for the purpose of celestial navigation, 33-35

Navy Tactical Data System
    Ships equipped with NTDS began arriving in the Pacific Fleet in the early 1960s, 126-128; used in a First Fleet firepower demonstration for President John F. Kennedy in June 1963, 130-134

Newell, Lieutenant Edward L., USN
    Discussed ideas for celestial navigation while serving in the battleship Utah (BB-31) in the late 1920s, 11

New Guinea
    Fire support by the destroyer Nicholas (DD-449) during the U.S. landings in April 1944, 68-69

New Jersey, USS (BB-62)
    In July 1954 the ship's surgeon performed an appendectomy on a crewman from the battleship Missouri (BB-63), 100-101

Nicaragua
    The United States maintained a military presence in the country up to the early 1930s, 21-22

Nicholas, USS (DD-449)
    Ship that had a superb combat record in the Solomon Islands in World War II, 67; gunfire support operations off New Guinea in 1944, 68-69; visit to the Admiralty Islands in 1944, 69; in November 1944 the Nicholas sank the Japanese submarine I-38, which was armed with Kaiten torpedoes, 69-73; wartime contributions by various crew members, 73

Nitro, USS (AE-2)
    Traveled widely in the mid-1930s while transporting ammunition for fleet use, 27-28, 30-31, 109; did mid-Pacific survey work at Wake Island in the mid-1930s, 28-29

Noble, Rear Admiral Albert G., USN (USNA, 1917)
    Capable officer who was involved in a variety of duties in his career, 40; as a task group commander in 1944 during the New Guinea operation, 68-69

Norfolk Navy Yard
    Overhauled the destroyer Overton, 1933-34, 27

Norfolk, Virginia
    Supervision of shore patrol for sailors ashore on liberty in the late 1930s, 41; as commander in Chief Atlantic Fleet in 1954, Admiral Jerauld Wright visited the battleship Missouri (BB-63) before she departed Norfolk for inactivation on the West Coast, 105

North, Captain James Robert, USN (USNA, 1935)
Gained ship-handling experience as executive officer of the battleship Missouri (BB-63) in the mid-1950s, 92-93; promotion to captain in the summer of 1954, 103-104; supervision of the inactivation of the Missouri in 1954, 106-107

Oriskany, USS (CVA-34)
In the early 1960s became one of the first NTDS-equipped warships to operate in the Pacific Fleet, 127; participated in a First Fleet firepower demonstration for President John Kennedy in June 1963, 130-134

Overesch, Captain Harvey E., USN (USNA, 1915)
Served as Commander Destroyer Division Ten in 1941, 58; overhaul of aptitude evaluations while serving as Naval Academy commandant of midshipmen in the early 1940s, 62

Overton, USS (DD-239)
Camaraderie among the crew in the early 1930s, 20; role as part of the Special Service Squadron operating in the Caribbean in the early 1930s, 21-26; overhauled at the Norfolk Navy Yard, 1933-34, 27

Panama
Role of aircraft carriers in the U.S. Navy's Fleet Problem IX in the Panama area in January 1929, 9; supervision of shore patrol for sailors ashore on liberty in the late 1930s, 39, 42

Panama Canal
Transits of the canal by the battleship Missouri (BB-63) in 1954 and 1986, 111-112

Parsons, Lieutenant Commander William Sterling, USN (USNA, 1922)
As executive officer of the destroyer Aylwin (DD-355) in the late 1930s, devised a tactic for night search, 93-94

Pearl Harbor, Hawaii
In 1939 the U.S. Fleet established a Hawaiian Detachment based at Pearl, 49-50, 52; In 1941 many of the Army Air Corps pilots stationed near Pearl were deployed elsewhere in Hawaii, 50; Japanese attack in 1941, 50-52; destroyers of the Hawaiian Detachment conducted a target practice against drones in 1941, 53-54, 60

Philippine Islands
As base commander at Subic Bay in the late 1950s, Keith used a trick to demonstrate to CinCPac the need for a certain fire station, 119-120; trial of individuals for stealing an LST in the Philippines in the late 1950s, 122; administration of justice in the late 1950s, 125

Portugal
The battleship Missouri (BB-63) visited the port of Lisbon during a midshipman training cruise in 1954, 98-99

Pratt, Albert
    As Assistant Secretary of the Navy in the mid-1950s, he investigated a case in which a Naval Academy midshipman was accused of cheating, 114-116

Presidential Aides
    The seniority of White House naval aides dropped when Dwight Eisenhower became President in 1953, 6-7; Rear Admiral Robert Dennison apparently put President Harry S. Truman up to heckling the skipper of the battleship <u>Iowa</u> (BB-61) in 1951, 117-118; Captain Tazewell Shepherd was involved in making arrangements for President John Kennedy to witness a First Fleet firepower demonstration in 1963, 131

Promotion of Officers
    Preparation for promotion examinations in the mid-1930s, 34-35; in 1954 Keith went to bat for his executive officer, J. R. North, to get him promoted to captain, 103-104

Puerto Rico
    Visited by the battleship <u>Arizona</u> (BB-39) with President Herbert Hoover on board in March 1931, 13

<u>Queen Elizabeth</u> (British Passenger Liner)
    Called at Cherbourg, France, in July 1954 with British Prime Minister Winston Churchill on board, 97-98

Refueling
    Coaling of the battleship <u>Texas</u> (BB-35) during a midshipman cruise in the mid-1920s, 2; fueling at sea done during fleet exercises in the late 1930s, 43-44; midshipmen conned the battleship <u>Missouri</u> (BB-63) for replenishment at sea in the summer of 1954, 99-100

Rescue at Sea
    The destroyer <u>Cushing</u> (DD-376) conducted experiments with life rafts in the Hawaii area in 1941, 56-57

Richardson, Admiral James O., USN (USNA, 1902)
    U.S. Fleet Commander in Chief who was relieved in early 1941 because of policy differences with President Franklin D. Roosevelt, 54-55

Rio de Janeiro, Brazil
    Visited by President-elect Herbert Hoover on board the battleship <u>Utah</u> (BB-31) in December 1928, 7-8

Sabin, Lieutenant Commander Lorenzo S., Jr., USN (USNA, 1921)
    Service on the Base Force staff during exercises in the late 1930s, 43, 45; recollections concerning Admiral J. O. Richardson, 55-56

San Francisco, California
    A pilot bringing the battleship <u>Missouri</u> (BB-63) into San Francisco in 1954 did a poor job of judging the current, 109-110; many people from San Francisco visited the <u>Missouri</u>, 110

St. John's College, Annapolis, Maryland
    During World War II the Naval Academy conducted a study on the feasibility of putting a Naval Reserve training unit at St. John's, 65-66

<u>**Saratoga**</u>**, USS (CV-3)**
    Role of in the U.S. Navy's Fleet Problem IX in the Panama area in January 1929, 9

Seattle, Washington
    Visited by the battleship <u>Missouri</u> (BB-63) on her way to inactivation in 1954, 113-114

Shepherd, Captain Tazewell T., Jr., USN (USNA, 1943)
    As naval aide to the President, was involved in making arrangements for John Kennedy to witness a First Fleet firepower demonstration in 1963, 131

Sherman, Admiral Forrest P., USN (USNA, 1918)
    Service on the staff of Commander in Chief U.S. Fleet in the late 1930s, 38-39, 42; friendliness toward Keith, 40

Ship Handing
    Handling characteristics of the battleship <u>Missouri</u> (BB-63) in shallow water, 92-95; a pilot bringing the <u>Missouri</u>. into San Francisco in 1954 did a poor job of judging the current, 109-110

Shore Bombardment
    Fire support by the destroyer <u>Nicholas</u> (DD-449) during the Aitape landings on New Guinea in April 1944, 68-69

Shore Patrol
    In Kiel, Germany, in 1929, 10; supervised by the Base Force during the late 1930s, 38-39, 41-43; in 1939 the commandant of the Mare Island Navy Yard was concerned about excess drinking by sailors on liberty in Vallejo, California, 47-48

Silver Services
    The state of Missouri presented silver to the two battleships named for the state, BB-11 and BB-63, 108-109

Small, Captain Ernest G., USN (USNA, 1912)
    As a destroyer division commander in 1940-41, observed a target practice firing against drones, 53-54, 60; conducted a gunnery school on board his flagship <u>Drayton</u> (DD-366), 60; served as a department head at the Naval Academy in 1941, 59-61

Smedberg, Rear Admiral William R. III, USN (USNA, 1926)
As Naval Academy superintendent during the mid-1950s showed Keith a scrapbook dealing with his time as commanding officer of the battleship Iowa (BB-61), 117-118

Smith, Lieutenant (j.g.) James Stuart, Jr., USN (USNA, 1925)
Served as a turret officer in the battleship Arizona (BB-39) in the early 1930s, 14-15

Sonar
In November 1944 the destroyer Nicholas (DD-449) used sonar to sink the Japanese submarine I-38, which was armed with Kaiten torpedoes, 69-73; experiments in the late 1950s with a sonobuoy-equipped drone helicopter for ASW, 118-119; drone helos were part of a firepower demonstration in 1963, 132

South America
Herbert Hoover made a goodwill tour of the continent after his election as President in 1928, 5-9, 12

Special Service Squadron
U.S. Navy ships that represented U.S. interests in the Caribbean in the early 1930s, 21-26

State Department
As U.S. ambassador to the Philippines in the late 1950s, Charles Bohlen was involved in negotiations about Filipino jurisdiction in legal cases, 125; in 1959 a wide number of individuals was authorized to sign messages on behalf of the Secretary of State, 129

Stewart, James
Popular movie actor who visited the battleship Missouri, (BB-63) at Long Beach in 1954, 110-111

Subic Bay, Philippine Islands
As base commander in the late 1950s, Keith employed a ruse to demonstrate to CinCPac the need for a certain fire station, 119-120; trial of individuals for stealing an LST in the Philippines in the late 1950s, 122

Surveying
The ammunition ship Nitro (AE-2) did mid-Pacific survey work around Wake Island in the mid-1930s, 28-29

Suturowski, Chief Fire Controlman Edward, USN
Handled fire control for the gun battery of the destroyer Aylwin (DD-355) in 1941, 52; attended Keith's retirement ceremony in 1964, 134

Swift, Major General Innis G., USA (USMA, 1904)
As commanding general of the First Cavalry Division, visited the destroyer Nicholas (DD-449) in 1944, 69

Tactics
    As executive officer of the destroyer Aylwin (DD-355) in the late 1930s, Lieutenant Commander William S. Parsons devised a tactic for night search, 93-94

Target Practice
    Firing of by the battleship Arizona (BB-39) in the early 1930s, 18-20; destroyers of the Hawaiian Detachment conducted a target practice against drones in 1941, 53-54, 60

Taylor, Rear Admiral Edmund B., USN (USNA, 1925)
    Commanded the destroyer Duncan (DD-485) when she was sunk off Guadalcanal in October 1942, 59; was the base commander at Guantanamo Bay, Cuba, in the mid-1950s, 95

Texas, USS (BB-35)
    Still burned coal prior to her modernization in the mid1920s, 2; firing of her 14-inch guns during night battle practice in the late 1920s, 107-108

Thomson, Earl W.
    Long-time Naval Academy physics professor who was less than impressive in the use of televised instruction in the early 1950s, 89-90

Thomson, Commander Thaddeus A., Jr., USN (USNA, 1907)
    Was difficult and demanding as executive officer of the battleship Arizona (BB-39) in the early 1930s, 13-16; as executive officer at the Naval Academy in the 1920s, 14-15

Tisdale, Captain Mahlon S., USN (USNA, 1912)
    Service on the Base Force staff in the late 1930s, 45; served as commandant of midshipmen at the Naval Academy in 1941-42 until he went to sea duty, 60-62

Torpedoes
    In November 1944 the destroyer Nicholas (DD-449) sank the Japanese submarine I-38, which was armed with Kaiten torpedoes, 69-73; experiments in the late 1950s with a torpedo-equipped drone helicopter for ASWI 118-119

Towers, USS (DDG-9)
    Keith spoke at the commissioning of this guided missile destroyer in 1961, 128

Train, Captain Charles Russell, USN (USNA, 1900)
    Commanded the battleship Utah (BB-31) in the late 1920s, 3-5; served as presidential naval aide in the early 1930s, 6

Training
    Role of aircraft carriers in the U.S. Navy's Fleet Problem IX in the Panama area in January 1929, 9; Firing of target practice by the battleship Arizona (BB-39) in the early 1930s, 18-20; damage control training during battle problems conducted in the

Hawaiian Detachment in 1939-40, 52-53; destroyers of the Hawaiian Detachment conducted a target practice against drones in 1941, 53-54, 60; training of the crew of the destroyer Herbert J. Thomas (DD-833) in 1945 for possible encounters with kamikazes, 74-75; installation of Naval Reserve training armories throughout the country shortly after World War II, 77; the battleship Missouri (BB-63) made a midshipman training cruise to France and Portugal in the summer of 1954, 97-105, 109

Truman, Harry S.
A man claiming to be from President Truman's home town visited the battleship Missouri (BB-63) in 1954, 110; when the battleship Iowa (BB-61) was recommissioned in 1951, Truman challenged her skipper's claim as to the size of the ship, 117-118

Turner, USS (DD-834)
Served as flagship of Destroyer Division 17 during public visiting in Washington, D.C., in the autumn of 1945, 75-76

Turrets
Firing of in the battleship Arizona (BB-39) in the early 1930s, 18-20

United Nations
Negotiating with the North Koreans was difficult and frustrating for U.N. representatives in the early 1960s, 128-129

Utah, USS (BB-31/AG-16)
Had a poor reputation among Naval Academy graduates in the late 1920s, 3-4; Captain Charles R. Train as commanding officer in the late 1920s, 3-5; training routine in the late 1920s, 4, 20; had President-elect Herbert Hoover on board during part of his goodwill trip to South America in late 1928, 5-9, 12; participated in Fleet Problem IX in the Panama area in January 1929, 9; cruise to Germany and France in the summer of 1929, 10; officers of the deck, 11-12; modernization in the early 1930s, 12-13; sports teams, 41; role in the late 1930s as an experimental gunnery ship, 46

Vallejo, California
In 1939 the commandant of the Mare Island Navy Yard was concerned about the excess drinking by sailors on liberty in Vallejo, 47-48

Vietnam War
Admiral Don Felt's comments in the early 1960s on the potential use of various tools in the Vietnam War, 127-128

Wake Island
The ammunition ship Nitro (AE-2) did mid-Pacific survey work around the island in the mid-1930s, 28-29

Washington, D.C.
The destroyer Turner (DD-834) served as flagship of Destroyer Division 17 during public visiting in Washington in the autumn of 1945, 75-76

Watts, Rear Admiral William Carleton, USN (USNA, 1898)
Commanded the Base Force, which supported the U.S. Fleet in the late 1930s, 37

Weinberger, Caspar
As Secretary of Defense, he spoke at the recommissioning of the battleship Missouri (BB-63) in 1986, 106-107

Welles, Sumner
Served as U.S. ambassador to Cuba in 1933, during the sergeants' revolt there, 24-26

White House
See Presidential Aides

Williamsburg, USS (AGC-369)
Ceased service as the presidential yacht in the early 1950s because Milton Eisenhower convinced his brother Dwight she was an unnecessary luxury, 86

Wright, Admiral Jerauld, USN (USNA, 1918)
As Commander in Chief Atlantic Fleet in 1954, visited the battleship Missouri (BB-63) before she departed Norfolk for inactivation on the West Coast, 105

Wright, USS (AV-1)
Tender received the pick of aviator players for her baseball team in the late 1930s, 41